Fresh Memories
A Daily Report of My Life in Seoul, Korea

by
Daisy W. Goodwin

Published by:
Divine Life Publications
P.O. Box 31099
Capitol Heights, MD 20731

Copyright © 2001
Daisy W. Goodwin

All rights reserved. No part of this book may be reproduced in any form, except for the inclusion of brief quotations in a review, without permission in writing from the author or publisher.

ISBN: 0-9679367-4-8

Library of Congress Control Number: 2001119857

Printed in the United States by:
Morris Publishing
3212 East Highway 30
Kearney, NE 68847

TO:

Octavia, Gerard & Tiffany

Cover:
Design on silk by the author

Prologue

As I reflect back on my early efforts to educate children in many classrooms in which I have taught, I recall many challenging and turbulent assignments over the years.

My first assignment as a teacher was in a classroom of black students in Baltimore, Maryland. At the same time, I was enrolled in an art school in the city. One evening, while attending class at the art school, I perused the cluttered bulletin board and my attention was drawn to an ad for teachers in Prince George's County, Maryland.

Because I was unhappy in my position at the time, I decided to apply for the Prince George's County position and I was accepted. However, things were no better in the integrated system in Prince George's County than they had been in Baltimore. Still, I taught in the County system for ten years before moving to and applying for a teaching position in Northern Virginia.

In the position in Northern Virginia, I was assigned to a school in a predominantly white and affluent community. Essentially, the parents ran the school and the children ran the classrooms. Both parents and students did an outstanding job of keeping the administrators and teachers on their toes. Administrators catered to the community for fear of losing their jobs. I was not happy in this environment either. So, after ten years in Northern Virginia, I decided to apply for a position with the Department of Defense Dependent Schools(DODDS).

I learned about DODDS through several Overseas Education Association conventions I had attended. I admired their teaching philosophy, their dedication, and their organizational ability. Since I had to teach because teaching was my profession, I decided to make the most of any opportunity that came my way. So, there I was in Seoul, Korea. The experience was overwhelmingly fulfilling and a great opportunity.

While in Korea, I kept a journal of my daily activities, and that is where the idea of making my journal into a book struck me. No one, as far as I know, has written a book on life in DODDS. We read about military service people, but very little about teachers who serve the children of service people.

Some of the names of persons in this book are fictitious.

1 August 1990

The telephone rang at about 7 p.m. on the evening of August 1, 1990. I could tell right away from the voice on the other end that it was a call from Korea. It was Ms. Ridgely, assistant principal of the Seoul American Elementary School, who called to assure me that two greeters would meet me at Kimpo Airport bearing a sign with my name on it. We talked very briefly and after she wished me a safe and good flight, we hung up. The call was what I needed to alleviate my fears of landing in a strange land with no confirmation that my travel plans had been received.

Shortly afterwards, Jenny, my sister, called to tell me that she was coming over. She, Sean and Jennifer, her son and daughter, came to my house laden with several bags. I was delighted when Jenny produced a plastic bag containing several items and presented them to me one at a time. The first was a *Bon Voyage* card, the second, a bound black journal to record my daily activities and thoughts, the third, a bag of candy and lastly, a paperback novel. This was just like Jenny, empathetic and thoughtful. By this time my daughter, Tavia and my granddaughter, Tia, arrived home. We all took a stroll within Harvey Circle and around the Circle.

After returning to the house, we popped a bottle of champagne and toasted my safety, a successful trip and job relocation. We spent a few more precious moments together and the Boyes' left, Jennifer and Jenny in my car and Sean in theirs. Jennifer was going to keep my car while I was away.

I gave Tavia some last minute instructions, then Gerald, Tavia, Tia and I gathered in my room for prayer. Then we all retired to bed.

The night was a restful one. I awakened fifteen minutes before the alarm sounded at 4:30 a.m. I dressed and drank a cup of coffee. This would be my last day at home for approximately eleven months.

2 August 1990

On our way to Dulles Airport, we stopped for gas and then proceeded to the automatic teller machine for some money. The traffic on 395 was slow and I was becoming anxious. The clock read 6:35 a.m. and I was to be at the airport at 7 a.m. I whispered a prayer and put my mind at ease for God had allowed everything to go smoothly up to this point and I knew He would not fail me now.

We arrived at the airport at 7:45 and I boarded the plane to San Francisco. Thoughts of home, family, job, friends and Korea crossed my mind, but I dismissed them quickly to concentrate on reading a magazine between watching an in-flight movie which featured James Earl Jones as one of the stars. The title was *The Hunt for Red October*.

The plane touched down at San Francisco Airport a little ahead of time. This gave me ample time to move about the airport to the next point of departure. After about an hour's wait, we were informed that our plane was *missing* and that they had to *find* another. That sounded scary. We were informed that we would be boarding around one and a half hours later at another gate.

There was a large group of Korean children waiting for the same flight. I was most impressed with their very fine conduct. They made themselves content by playing quiet games, writing and talking with little or no adult supervision. I hoped with all my heart that this would be the type of children that I would be assigned.

We boarded the plane at approximately 3 p.m. It was now our seventh hour of flight over the Pacific Ocean. I have just finished watching a movie, having a snack and responding to two surveys sent to me from Northern Virginia school system. The airplane was very lively. Passengers were walking about stretching their legs and the children were playing.

As we approached the other side of the world, I looked out the window and marveled at the beautiful sight. It was indeed a scene of a *land of morning calm.* It was something to behold, the blue, pink and white sky.

3 August 1990

After eleven hours in the sky, we landed safely at Kimpo Airport at 6:45 p.m. My sponsors (meeter/greeters) were nowhere to be found. I found out later that they thought that I was coming in on Northwest Airlines.

I was able to get the assistance of a passenger service person. We made a dozen calls before we finally got someone to tell me what to do and where I would be staying. I stood for over three hours in the airport terminal trying to find out what to do. We finally reached a Mr. Taney, principal at Seoul American High School, who directed me to the Hyatt Hotel where reservations had been made for me until Monday.

The hotel and the room are lovely. Seoul is very much like America. It is so strange to me and at the same time, familiar. At this point I feel much at ease. I watched President Bush on an English speaking television channel. He gave an up-to-date report on the Iran/Saudi Arabia/Kuwait situation.

4 August 1990

I slept well last night after watching a movie. I was, however, startled by a sound at my door at 4:30 a.m. I got up to check it out and found that someone had pushed the morning newspaper under my door. I went back to sleep and woke up again at 6:45 a.m. I got up, showered and dressed. I am staying on the 16th floor which is the Regency Center and it allows special treatment to its guests. I went down the hall to find that a scrumptious buffet breakfast was being served without additional charge. After eating, I returned to my room and received a call from Ivy Turner, a teacher from the States, who is staying on the fifth floor of the same hotel. I invited her to my room and we talked at length. We later went to Yongsan Base where we met Katie Zinns for lunch at the Oasis Restaurant in the Dragon Hill Lodge.

I returned to my hotel and napped. I was then awakened by a call from Rosa Ridgely, assistant principal at the Seoul American Elementary School. She was downstairs in the hotel lobby. I went downstairs to get her and Anne Nevens, my sponsor, because to get to my floor, one needed a key for the elevator. We rode to the 16th floor for a repast in the area where breakfast was served that morning. As with the breakfast, it was lovely. Rosa and Anne made me feel so much at home. They made me feel that I had made the right choice in becoming a part of DODDS, Department of Defense Dependant Schools.

5 August 1990

I awakened a couple of times during the night. I finally got up at 6:30, dressed and watched a religious program on television from Youngstown, Ohio. The pastor was Dr. Wagner, a black minister leading a large black congregation. The gospel music was very inspiring. Prior to watching the telecast, I listened to the morning news which included the invasion of Kuwait by Iraq and Mayor Barry's drug perjury trial. I then went to breakfast in the lounge. Later I was able to get a ride to the 11:30 Gospel Service. It was very much like home with the drums and tambourines accompanying the choir, very high spirited. The congregation was 99 percent black. After service, I walked to the main exchange area to get a cab where I lunched again at the Oasis.

6 August 1990

I arose early as usual. I received a call from Rosa Ridgely informing me that she would come to pick me up to assist me with getting an I.D. card, ration card and a BOQ (Bachelor Officers' Quarters). This was quite an ordeal going from building to building. I also met the principal, Beatrice Knox and the secretary, Jan. We could not get into the BOQ right away so we had to make arrangements to stay at the Dragon Hill Lodge on base. We then spent time in a shopping area called Itaewan (ee-tay-won). The merchants made use of every foot of space. There were shops on the street level, the basement, upstairs, down alleys and vendors on the streets. I had never seen anything like it before. It was interesting that when a motorist almost makes another have an accident, they will stop their cars in the middle of the street and fight. We saw this while downtown. Otherwise, the people are gentle and very polite.

Rosa and I had lunch and then spent several hours in the hotel casino. I spent the time playing the nickel slots. After awhile, I decided to forgo this activity because it was taxing on my legs. I visited Rosa's apartment which offers an overwhelming view of the city. She had lovely furniture. On returning from her apartment, we saw military police bracing themselves for a possible riot. I went to my hotel room very tired, but managed to watch a T.V. special featuring Mary Reeves and other rock and roll singers of the sixties.

7 August 1990

I awakened early, dressed, and called Sam Hopkins, a new DODDS teacher, to join me for breakfast on my floor. Today we were to check out of the Hyatt Regency and into Dragon Hill Lodge located on the base. We drove to Osan Base 30 miles away to apply for advance pay because hotel meals and taxi expenses were piling up. Osan Base seemed to be more modern than Yongsan. The shopping areas seemed less crowded and trees shaded the sidewalk.

After returning from Osan, I stopped at the recreation center to send a Marsgram to Jenny and Tavia.

8 August 1990

Most of this day was relatively quiet. Selena, another DODDS teacher, Sam and I had breakfast at the Oasis, a restaurant in our hotel, *Dragon Hill*, then proceeded to do some more settling of business. We checked on the status of the BOQ, applied for a ration card, applied for direct payroll deposit and mailed more Marsgrams. Marsgrams are short messages of not more than thirty words which the Army will either phone or mail to a friend or a relative in the States in two days at no charge. When we returned to the hotel, I wrote a couple of letters and then I went to Burger King for lunch. While there it rained quite heavily. We heard that just prior to our arrival that the monsoon season had just ended. It had rained for forty-five consecutive days.

9 August 1990

Today was Mama's birthday. Had she lived she would have been eighty-five years old. Perhaps it was the memories of her that kept me awake most of the night. I think of her often. I vowed that her spirit would live forever in me. I arose very early and joined Selena and Sam for breakfast at the Oasis. From there we took the bus to Osan for more processing. We returned to the base and took care of some more preparations for permanent housing and work.

All day has been dry. The morning was cool and calm, thus the slogan for Korea, *The Land of the Morning Calm*. I retired to my room about 5 p.m. and have spent the rest of the evening here. My temporary lodging in the hotel is excellent. I have a sitting area, a dining area, a kitchenette with a microwave oven, and the T.V. has a VCR. I am grateful to Jenny for providing me with packets of coffee because now I can make a pot of coffee in my room.

10 August 1990

I slept a little better last night. I awoke about 5:30 a.m. and made breakfast. Sam and Selena came over and we helped Selena with filling out her travel voucher. Selena and I then went downstairs to the hair care center to have our hair styled. The cost was very reasonable for a shampoo, deep conditioner and set. The center also did manicures, facials and body massages. Afterwards, we went to the post office to try to open my mail box, but with no success. How frustrating! We returned to the hotel, made some purchases at the Post Exchange in the hotel and returned to our rooms with intentions of doing our laundry later. We did not. We became lazy.

We went out later to the bank and to browse around the library and main exchange. Rosa came in while we were at the library and informed me that she had waiting in the car a teacher from Silver Spring, Maryland. So, I went out to meet her and found her to be very friendly.

After returning to the hotel we went to Bently's Lounge which featured a happy hour with food (tacos, etc.). It must be the place where the military men go for a free meal and to hang out. They were there, loud as ever. I decided to return to my room for the evening. I watched television and fell asleep.

11 August 1990

    I awakened a couple of times during the night, then got up at approximately 6:30 a.m. I showered and decided to have breakfast downstairs in the hotel's Oasis Room. I called Sam and Selena to find out what they would be doing today. Sam was going to a softball tournament and Selena's sponsors were taking her out. Since I wouldn't have either's company for the day I had to find something to do on my own. I then recalled that at Gospel Service last Sunday it was announced that the Women's Support Group was having a retreat. I had thrown away my program, so I didn't know what time nor where, but I had to find out. I finished breakfast and went walking down the street. I recognized a serviceman who was in church on Sunday and I asked him. He didn't know, but he referred me to Chaplain Easton whom he said was still having breakfast in the Greenstreet Room of the hotel.

    As I approached the hotel, who was coming out? --- Chaplain Easton. He told me to go by cab to the 8th Army Retreat Center to the conference room. I did, and was I glad. Just like the retreat that I organized at Prince William Forest Park in Virginia, it was indeed a mountaintop experience. Several of the ladies that I had seen and met at church on Sunday were there. They welcomed me with opened arms. The speakers were outstanding -- every one. The speakers were Chaplain Easton, Elder McMichael, Paula Riff, Marie Knight and Helen Jones. They spoke on such topics as marriage, parenting, singles, encouragement and Christian dress respectively. They fed us well. I missed breakfast, but the snacks, lunch and dinner were great. We were given helpful hand-outs. The fellowship among the participants was overwhelming. I returned to the hotel at about 8 p.m.

13 August 1990

Today I moved from Dragon Hill Lodge to my bachelor officers quarters. Before doing that, Selena and I went to take care of some other business. We arranged to have our telephones installed and learned it would take up to six weeks. We sent two Marsgrams to our families in the States. We also selected two tours to go on in the next two weeks.

I checked out of my room, went to borrow household items that I would need until mine arrived from the States. My BOQ had to be inspected by me and an inspection sheet signed. It was nice. I could live with it. We then had lunch at Burger King. Yes, there are Burger Kings here as well as Wendy's, Kentucky Fried Chicken and Denny's.

This evening Selena, Kathy Jannis, a DODDS teacher and I went to Itaewan, a shopping district not far from where we live. I purchased a handbag. I planned to return to purchase some shoes to match the bag, some Korean masks and a shale/mother-of-pearl telephone. I returned to my BOQ, had a light snack and finished cleaning my bedroom and bathroom. I also put away things from my luggage. I have a television which I am thankful for since I did not ship one.

14 August 1990

I got up at 5 a.m. and cleaned the kitchen. I drank a couple of cups of coffee. When I noticed that it was raining quite heavily, I started to dress as quickly as I could because I was to meet Sam and Kathy at Dragon Hill Lodge to go to Osan to file for reimbursement of our hotel expenses. On the way to Osan there was a terrible accident. A car had broken through a rail and went down an embankment. Then a funny thing happened. Out of the blue I began to think of Mama. I tried to imagine her pain and agony. I tried hard to hold back the tears. I thought of the many years she suffered and I know not how much. Slowly the thoughts vanished.

We arrived at Osan Air Base and found Mr. Shields, the finance officer. He was patient and helpful. He even drove us to the bank. After taking care of business, we had a delicious pasta meal at La Cantina on the base. We then decided to get a taxi to the shopping district of Osan. It didn't have as much to offer as Itaewan, but I purchased two handbags for gifts. I saw several custom made shoe stores and decided that that would be my next purchase. As we walked, we noticed how conservatively dressed Korean people are. They do not wear short shorts nor halters. They don't sell them either. The women wear nice dresses, a blouse and skirt or top and knee length shorts. Men wear shirts and long pants or knee length shorts.

After our shopping, we went to the bus stop to wait for the bus. We waited about an hour and a half and when one came it was full. After waiting another hour we decided to get a taxi to the bus station to find out what was wrong. There was a delay in the bus returning from Yongsan. We waited another half hour before the bus finally came.

When I arrived at my BOQ I rested a few minutes, when there was a knock at the door. It was Selena. After she left I prepared to attend the Women's Support Group meeting at the chapel. As I was walking, Sharon, a member of the group, stopped and gave me a ride. When we arrived, the meeting was in progress. The group was discussing why Paula Riff, a DODDS teacher, should be president. She acknowledged her fault of being abrupt. She seemed cold to me, but warmed up when she found out that we were neighbors. The meeting ended with a baby shower for one of the members.

I was thinking today about not having to drive to work. My BOQ is about a five minute walk from school. HURRAY! No filling up at the gas station!!! No cleaning ice in the winter and no driving twenty-six miles round trip to and from work.

15 August 1990

I read in the paper that last year Koreans consumed 33,000 tons of dog meat and that there are 1,200 restaurants serving dog meat. Koreans resent reports that eating dog meat is shameful. I don't intend to eat any.

This is a good time in my life to be here. It gives me an opportunity to "step back" and take a look at my life, to sort of start over, to do things as I've always wanted to do. I feel that life has been preparing me for this moment. The trials, the hardships, my training, my joys have been polishing me to shine. I have no regrets. It gives me an opportunity to get away from Gerald and Tavia so that they can function and *grow* without my physical presence.

This day is a Korean holiday, Independence/Unification Day. During the week South Koreans are supposed to be allowed to visit North Korean friends and relatives. There was a riot at the border when students tried to demonstrate. The day before, the riot squad was at the main gate of the base when a car of dissidents wanted to come on base to talk to American officials. To me this was not unusual. We demonstrate almost weekly in the United States, too.

16 August 1990

This day was a very exciting day. The Army Community Services sponsored a newcomer's orientation that began with a refreshment time of coffee, juice, and pastries. We were welcomed and admonished to get out among the people, learn, and to be ambassadors for America. We were shown an excellent video on all the features of the base. We were given some additional information by Sara Whitt, family services manager. Prior to the session, we were given a wonderful welcome folder. After Sara's talk we were shown a great video on Seoul. We then took a twenty minute break to go to another room where representatives from the various agencies on the base were on hand to answer any questions we had. We returned to the meeting and we each received a coffee mug. Another highlight of the session was the Korean dancers. The first group danced a solemn honor dance, followed by a woman solo dancer, then a group of dancers who danced a folk type dance with a solo male dancer. It was lovely. Our final treat was an hour long tour of Seoul. The sights were interesting, overwhelming and fun. We saw temples, shopping areas, the business district, the Olympic stadium, commonfolk, rush hour traffic, etc. I took many pictures.

   Later in the afternoon I attended a farewell social for Minister Glenda Allen whom I met at the Women's Support Group Retreat. Babs Dorsey and I spent a short time at the affair because we were to meet with Ms. Goins, a Korean who is married to a black American, to go by subway to the Olympic Stadium for the World Baptist Alliance Congress. I was very excited to be riding the subway for the first time. It was similar to those in the United States, but so much more crowded. We arrived at the beautiful stadium and who should I see immediately, Reverend Crawford, Pastor of St. Paul's Baptist Church in Baltimore where Joyce, my niece, is a member. I looked around the auditorium and there in a reserved area on the first row of the arena was Reverend James Patterson, Reverend Faith Gill and Reverend Albert Runyon, clergy at my church in Virginia. The program consisted of a bell choir, two videos on Baptists in Latin America and in Africa, the National Baptist Congress Choir from the United States, a speech by a delegate from Burma, and a sermon by Reverend Charles Adams of Chicago on *Love*. One of the highlights of the session was when we all joined hands and people from around the world prayed. The spirit was high. One could feel it move from person to person. Another powerful prayer was offered by delegates from Africa.

17 August 1990

The 8th Army Command, Younsan Base, is the largest in Korea. In the 1950's the Korean War was raged. Every day the riot squad seem to be posted at the main gate ready for action. They are very young men -- they look more like teenagers. I feel quite safe, though.

I hired the services of a laundry lady and a housekeeper. The cost is $35.00 a month.

I had to borrow a watch from Selena because I did not have one nor a clock. After four days, I put it in my purse to return to her, but she wasn't at home when I visited her. Sam and I decided to brave the subway under my directions to go to a shopping area. Upon returning to the base, I ran into Selena and began to fish through my purse for her watch. It was not there! I didn't know where or how I could have lost it. I will have to go to the main exchange to purchase another and to find out the depreciation value of it. Selena said it cost $125.00 when she purchased it two years ago.

I was able to get Kathy Jannis to go with me by subway to the evening session of the World Baptist Alliance Congress. The singing was beautiful. One of the choirs was from India and the main speaker was from India as well. Her topic focused on love. Upon arriving back in Yongsan by subway, we found it very difficult to get a cab. The drivers would stop, look at us and drive on, so we had to walk home. This was about 11:30 p.m.

18 August 1990

I was very impressed with the clean and neat appearance of all the Koreans that I saw. I did see a bag lady in Osan who was rummaging through a trash can and another Korean sitting on the floor at the bottom of the steps in the subway. Another Korean man stopped to talk and try to help him. I admired his compassion.

When I got up on this morning I made a list of things I needed to do. On the top of my list was to check the cost of a Pulsar watch. I was told at the main exchange that a shipment would be coming in next Wednesday and they are priced at $50.00. After having a delicious lunch of soup and a salad at the Greenstreet Restaurant in Dragon Hill Lounge, I went over to Main Post to the Moyer Recreation Center to learn to weave a heart shaped basket. There were five of us and it took three and a half hours to weave the basket. It turned out nicely.

Before leaving the center, I called Faith Gill who was one of the members from Alston Street Baptist Church attending the World Baptist Alliance Congress. We talked at length. She asked that I write her at the church because she was interested in bringing her son to visit. She said that she was ready to return to the States because she missed her husband and son.

I returned to my BOQ, began to watch television and fell asleep. I was awakened by a knock at the door. It was Paula Riff, my neighbor and a teacher at the high school. She said she was checking on me since I wasn't at the chaplain's farewell dinner.

19 August 1990

Today was the day that Selena, Kathy, Sam and I went on a tour of Geumgoh Temple. We had planned to meet for breakfast at 7:30 a.m., but since we thought we were running late we stopped at the deli to get a pastry and coffee. We were under the impression that we were to be at the bus station fifty minutes early, then found out it should have been thirty minutes early. So, we actually had twenty minutes to spare.

The ride to the tomb took an hour. The guide was quite informative. We took pictures of the burial mounds, temples, keeper's house and ground workers and when we returned to the bus depot, we decided to do some shopping. I purchased three ornamental mirrors for my bathroom, a floral maroon vase for the living room and snack food.

I was in my ninth hour of fasting which began about 8:30 a.m. this morning. Since I missed Sunday morning Gospel Service I attended the evening service which consisted of praise, prayer and a sermonette.

20 August 1990

I awakened a little later than usual, I dressed and broke my fast at about 8:30 a.m. I had cold cereal, coffee, toast and apple sauce. It was raining quite heavily this morning. It has been raining quite frequently. I enjoyed the sound of the rain and I enjoyed watching it come down as I looked out from my living room window.

I went to school to see if my room assignment had been confirmed. It had. I went inside and was pleased to find my classroom quite spacious. I liked the two cushioned swivel desk chairs, one with arms and one without. I had a computer and a television, also. There was little blackboard space and no bulletin boards. I would have to make displays on the walls. I spent a few hours there. I had lunch and went on Main Post to have heels put on my shoes, have a pair of shoes made, put some film in for developing and to inquire about education courses at The Education Center being offered by the University of Maryland.

The rain finally stopped. I returned home and watched *Amen*. I also met two other fifth grade teachers, Ms. Canty and Mrs. Macklin.

21 August 1990

I did not sleep well at all last night and when this happens it signals that something unpleasant will happen the following day. I got up, dressed, had breakfast and checked my plans for the day. I then went to the school mailroom to check my box. I was elated to see a large envelope from Tavia. I took it to my classroom and went through the contents. The auto insurance was due in six days, so I had to arrange to have that paid. I called Tavia collect to find that she was doing okay. She informed me that Gerald wasn't doing well financially and that there was a possibility that his car may be repossessed. I sent money on the note last week and on another bill. I did not want to tell him that I had done this for fear that he would stop making payments. I hoped he could work things out.

It has been raining heavily all day. I had to go to the Army Services Building to get a Status of Forces Agreement stamp on my visa. This allows me further protection and recognition while living in a foreign country. I also picked up a non-combatant evaluation kit. It will be most helpful should I have to be evacuated from the country.

22 August 1990

This was the day I was waiting for. I reported to work at 7:25 a.m. We had a general orientation session. During this session when we introduced ourselves, I found out that there were three other teachers from Northern Virginia; Rene Ennis taught in Alexandria and lived on Frye Road, Doria Johns taught at Silverbrook Elementary School in Area 1 of Fairfax County and Missy Hill lived in Springfield. Most of the day was spent in meetings and health screening. I got little done in my room so I took quite a bit of work home. It started raining again but not as hard as yesterday.

23 August 1990

I arrived at work about 7:45 a.m., checked my mailbox and paid Nat Nalls 5,000 won for the lunch which we were to have at Lotte World. At 8 a.m. we met on grade level with Chloe Macklin, chairperson. Afterwards she took us on a tour of the school campus. I then returned to my room to work for about 45 minutes. At 11:30 a.m. twenty-six teachers boarded the subway to go to Lotte Department Store for an authentic Korean meal in a Korean setting. It was quite difficult sitting on the floor mats. Our meal consisted of fish eggs, kofu, kimchi, soup, fish, and other foods. People passed by, stopped, stared and laughed at us. I guess it was quite amusing to them seeing us trying to eat with chopsticks. The meal was delicious. We then went through a fabulous historical museum. The exhibitions were outstanding. We also saw a performance of dancers doing a farmers' dance. We walked on where we came to a skillful calligrapher. I had him to write my name in very stylized calligraphy. It cost 10,000 won, about $14.00. It was lovely. We were becoming tired, but as we were leaving the floor we paused to look out the window at Lotte World Amusement Park. It is similar to our Disneyland, complete with monorails, hot air balloons, water rides, etc. We arrived back at school at about 4:45 p.m. I gathered up material to work on at home.

I retired for about a half hour then went to the Embassy Club where the staffs of both the high school and the elementary school were invited. We were provided with roast beef, finger foods, cakes and a complimentary drink. I left early because I needed to get home to work on my school work.

24 August 1990

When the alarm went off at 5:30 a.m., I did not want to get up. When I did, I felt very tired and sore. My thumb was extremely sore. I noticed yesterday that it was swollen. When I arrived at work I put an antiseptic and two bandages on it. That helped. I also got a very bad headache. I don't get headaches often. The last one I had must have been about two years ago.

We had an early meeting and went to the cafeteria to see where pupils were to be seated and also to see where buses line up. The school has 45-50 buses. I spent several hours working in my room. A few students and their parents stopped by to see me.

After school I went to the beauty salon. Upon my return I took an alcohol bath to relieve my stiffness. It did help.

I thought about Stanley, my brother, this afternoon and how he has always wanted to go to the mountains. It is my goal to take him there when I return home next summer.

25 August 1990

I awakened to a sunny day. I did my usual reading and then prepared to go to have breakfast at the Oasis. I ordered a large breakfast of eggs, sausage, pancakes and coffee and wished I had not ordered such a hefty meal. I have not been particularly fond of breakfast foods anyway except for cold cereal, breads and applesauce. After breakfast I stopped in the casino to play the few nickels I had after telling myself that I would not patronize the machine room. Afterwards I went to the lounge area to read the daily paper I had just purchased. I then walked back to my BOQ and began to work on my schoolwork when someone knocked on my door. The telephone installation men had come to install my telephone. I was so happy. After they left I worked more and then walked over to Kathy's BOQ to meet with her to walk to the T.E.A.K.'s (Teachers Education Association of Korea) picnic. We traveled through some hilly terrain to get there. We were taking a shortcut. The spread of food was overwhelming and more and more came. I had two plates, one for the main dishes, and another for fruits and some desserts. We mingled awhile and returned by an easier route.

I thought of Mama and Daddy. Daddy's passing was very sad, but with Mama gone it was even sadder. I wished they could have lived a little longer. I've begun to cherish my family more.

I want to do all that I can to keep our bond strong. I missed Tia, my granddaughter. I prayed each day that she would grow strong in body, mind and spirit and in the admonition of God.

This evening I attended the first anniversary of the Youth Assembly of Yongsan, a group of beautiful black teenagers all adorned in beige blouses, mustard colored skirts, dark colored pants, paisley bow ties and paisley cummerbunds. Their guests were the Osan Choir from Osan Air Base and the Yongsan Gospeleers. After the service, dinner was served in the fellowship hall. It consisted of chicken, mashed potatoes and gravy, corn, string beans, cole slaw, rolls, cake and drinks. You don't go hungry here.

26 August 1990

One of my concerns as I left the States was whether I would hear good gospel preaching and singing. The services in Korea are as uplifting if not more than those I attended at home. Today, instead of attending service at Gospel Service in Memorial Chapel, I went to the Protestant Service at South Post Chapel. It was beautiful and lasted for only one hour. The chapel was a very large modern structure. The congregation was the opposite of Gospel Service, being 99 percent white. The scriptures were read by a very articulate black gentleman. They had a great bell choir which played so spiritually. The minister's sermon was thorough and thought-provoking and the parishioners were friendly. The people were loving and very Christianlike. I guess it is because we are all so far from home and we need that bonding, friendship and support. I looked across the congregation and saw Kathy Jannis. When the visitors were asked to stand, a young woman announced that she was from Quantico, Virginia. I saw her after service and she said that she had just resigned from the Marine Corps because she and her husband were apart so much. She said she was applying to be a substitute teacher at the elementary school.

At 2:30 I attended the 8th United States Army Band Concert in the Moyer Recreation Center. It was free as are most activities here. It was great. They played a medley of Stephen Foster tunes, a Korean folk song, *Comrades* and other military songs.

The military makes every effort to make you feel at home. Just about everything that we have in the U.S. we have here. One may get lonely for family and friends but not for the States or lack of the presence of the States.

27 August 1990

This was the first day of school for the children. I arrived at work at 6:40. Everyone was bustling around. I met each of the twenty-three children at the door with a handshake. Ben Keys was in another class until 1:30 when he realized he was in the wrong room. Because of a mix-up in location, I missed my 30-minute break. I also missed eating lunch, because I had to go back to the classroom to get Cole's lunch and while there a response person came in to get some information. Other than that the day went fine. I worked until 3:40. Our contract day is 7:40 - 2:30. After work I went to visit the district superintendent at his request. He informed me that the Fairfax County School System is the measuring rod for DODDS. He said that since many

DODDS in Korea are so isolated that only one year tours are offered, but he wished I would stay on for a couple of years.

28 August 1990

The second day went well. The only incident that occurred was when Wade, a student, mashed his finger in the door. So I had to assign someone to hold the door open for the class. The school has an enrollment of approximately 1400 pupils. Most of them ride the bus. After school we had our monthly faculty meeting and following that a T.E.A.K. meeting. I went home very tired from so much walking. It would get better I was assured. I have spent the rest of the evening at home doing schoolwork, reading and watching T.V. My classroom is in a three-room hut.

29 August 1990

I can leave my BOQ, walk a few yards down the street and cross the street and I am at work in three minutes. What a difference from the 40-mile and 26-mile round trips to work at home. I did not bring my car and am I glad. No filling up at the gas station and no cleaning ice from the car in winter. You have to take a test here to get a license but there are no rules in driving. Drivers put on turn signals when they turn, not before. They honk constantly. It is much like New York and Washington, D.C.

In Maryland and Virginia, I never saw any of my students or co-workers after school. Here, it is different. Co-workers live in the same building with me, attend the same church, shop in the commissary, etc. Every time I leave my BOQ, I see someone from work, church, etc. every time.

I went to the commissary for the first time. It was like the Gunston Plaza *Basics*. I intended to buy a month's allotment of food but ended up buying six bags. Luckily, I did. I had to get a taxi. The drivers here are not like those at home. They give little assistance. The driver took my bags from the cab and set them on the curb. I had to make three trips in order to get my groceries to my BOQ. Oh well, that was that.

I checked my weight and found out that I have lost six pounds since being here.

30 August 1990

I received my first pay. It was for three days. The day went along nicely. I signed up to have a Korean dress made. I learned to say three Korean expressions. I am going to try to learn a phrase a week. *"A kneng ha say yo"* means good morning, " *a kneng ka ha say-yo"* means good bye, and *"kam-se-ha-ne-dah"* means thank you.

When I woke up I could hear the rain. When it rains here, it rains hard and long. The children had to run from building to building. After work I went to pick up my permanent ration card. Afterwards I went to the Hispanic Festival at the Dragon Hill. There were displays representing countries of the Hispanic world. There was also food that you could sample for $1.50 a dish or sample. In the ballroom the technicians were setting up the band equipment. When it was 5:30 I decided to go back to my BOQ until 7 p.m. when the band would begin to perform. When I got home, I laid down and fell asleep. When I woke up it was 8:15 so I decided against it. It was late and I don't like to go out at night alone.

1 September 1990

It rained again. I went to Chosun, a gift store, where I purchased two covered teacups to send stateside along with two silk pouches for the residents of Pendleton House, a senior citizens home in Alexandria. By this time, it was time to go to Moyer Recreation Center where the tour bus leaves to take us to the wharf where the boat leaves. I signed up on Thursday to take the Hans River boat ride. I wasn't sure about the ride because it had been raining very heavily and weather warnings of 40 miles per hour winds north of Taegu were telecast for the weekend. Despite all, the trip was lovely. The boat was spacious and comfortable. I saw a young Korean woman who was on the tour of the temple with me two weeks ago. She remembered me. I met two other young Korean women who were training to be tour guides. They sat with me and talked at length. We photographed each other. They told me that they learned to speak English in high school. After leaving the boat, we boarded a bus to tour the Seoul Sports Complex. It is enormous. There was a building for boxing, one for weight lifting, one for swimming, an arena for baseball, an arena for tennis, an arena for soccer and many other features. Many schoolchildren were swimming in the pool. It costs 4,000 won to use the facility.

As I walked to my BOQ, I thought, this would be home for the next ten months. I didn't miss my job or Virginia, but I did miss my family. I hoped they were doing well. I wished somehow they could share this new life with me. It was amazing. I hoped it wouldn't change. After arriving home, I prepared a meal, decided what I would wear to church and then watched *Star Search*.

2 September 1990

A month ago, I departed home to come to Korea. It is Sunday and I am in my 21st hour of my 24 hour fast. I checked my weight and I have lost 5 ½ lbs.

When I awakened, this morning, the ground was dry. I debated whether or not to carry my umbrella. I decided to carry one when I remembered that weather alerts are in effect until Sunday because of the typhoon that is moving north of Taegu. It began to rain hard. I enjoy the sound of the rain, though.

I attended the Protestant Service at South Post Chapel. The school district superintendent sang in the choir. His wife was in the audience. I didn't see anyone else that I recognized other than the black gentleman who read scripture last Sunday. The minister's text came from a song entitled *On Eagle's Wings*. He said that in our lowest periods and moments, God bears us up on eagles wings, breathes a breath of life and lets us shine through like the sun. In my life I've found that is true. As long as there is a tomorrow, as long as one believes in himself and God and perseveres he can make it. One must never give up hope.

After leaving the Protestant Service at 11:30 a.m. I walked over to Main Post to Gospel Service at Memorial Chapel. It was supposed to start at 11:15. Babs Dorsey, her husband and Mother Ball were ushering. The new pastor, Reverend Mangey, preached a dynamic sermon from I Corinthian 11:17 - 27, (*The Lord's Supper*). Reverend Mangey is both spiritual and entertaining. The Protestant Service had communion and so did the Gospel Service. Many parishioners in the Protestant Service broke their bread wafer before eating it because the Bible says that Jesus broke the bread. In the Gospel Service, Reverend Mangey says <u>we</u> <u>are</u> <u>not</u> to break the bread because the Bible says <u>Jesus</u> <u>broke</u> the bread, gave it to his disciples and told them to eat it, all of it.

On the way home, I stopped at Moyer Recreation Center to rest my feet. I saw flyers advertising pottery making and drybrush painting on pottery. I decided to put both classes on my calendar. While I was writing, the sun came out, and then it was gone; funny weather.

When I arrived home I made a shrimp salad and a waldorf salad. I prepared something else to go with it. I needed and wanted to lose a few more pounds. I still drank my lemon water.

I watched *The Women of Brewster Street* tonight. There comes a time in our lives that we must tear down walls, whether they are walls of debt, walls of loneliness, walls of unfair treatment, walls of clinging too closely or whatever. We must work to alleviate those things that eat at us. I have a feeling that some wall of some kind will always be with us, but we must continue to tear them down as long as we can. The walls of Germany came down, others can, too.

3 September 1990

I have been in Korea one month. This was Labor Day and many activities have been planned. After my usual morning reading, I went to the field to watch two softball games. The home team won the first game 3-0 and the other team won the second 9-4. I returned home, had a quick lunch and then went to Main Post where many activities were going on. The highlight of the festivities was a chili cook-off. Fourteen groups participated. I was too full to try any of the chili. There were many booths with displays and game booths for the children. A couple of hard rock bands provided music. I stopped at the voter booth to fill out a voter absentee ballot for Virginia. I saw many of my students and their parents. There was also a fashion show. I went inside and played five games of bingo at 50¢ a card. I then went upstairs to the deck where I had an excellent view of all the activities going on below. I stayed on Main Post until about 3:50, then returned to South Base. On the way I noticed that there was a high school football field. As I approached the field I noticed it was empty and the game was over so I decided to continue on to Dragon Hill Lodge. The pianist was performing in the lobby. I sat and listened until she took her break.

There are many caterpillars in Korea. My BOQ is at the end of the hall near an open door and so they creep into the hallway and often under the door and into the apartment. I have tried to close the door, but can't. I had to get someone to close the outside door in an effort to keep the creatures out. Since I have no insect spray, I poured some ammonia along the base of the door to keep them out. This did the job.

4 September 1990

I arrived at school a little later this morning for no reason at all. The day went nicely. There was a long meeting after school, but that's all a part of the job. I went to my mailbox and found a card from Marian, my sister. Marian included a newspaper clipping and picture announcing, her daughter, Amira's wedding. I was happy for her. I was sure it would be a lovely wedding. I regretted that I would not be able to attend, I hoped some members of my family would go.

In the evening I attended the Women's Support Group meeting at Memorial Chapel. This was the first meeting for the new president, my neighbor who teaches at the high school. She came up with the theme for the group which is "Know Yourself, Know Someone Else." The philosophy behind this was that if we seek to understand what is going on inside of us and in our lives, this would enable us to help and understand others. The meeting was very fruitful. We planned to have a tape ministry for people who could not come to church. We planned to move to a larger meeting area because we felt that our group meetings would be so supportively strong that we would draw other women.

5 September 1990

This was the day that I was hoping to receive my *hold baggage*, boxes that I had shipped over on July 30th, but no such luck. The crisis in the Middle East was really interfering with overseas transportation.

I received two letters from Jenny. She assures me that everything at home is alright.

The day at work was a regular one. I went to the Korean culture teacher's room to be fitted for a hanbok, a two-piece Korean dress. It will cost over a hundred dollars, but I did want something authentic. I will earn my money back because I plan to have a Korean culture presentation similar to my African mask presentation which earned money for me.

I agreed to run as a candidate for Teacher Education Association of Korea representative. I am sure that with my credentials I can win.

I was selected to participate in the Study of Teacher Training.

We had a math workshop after work where the math resource person explained to us the math program and materials. It was quite informative. During the session we munched on all kinds of Korean packaged snacks and drank Coke.

I live in a BOQ. A BOQ is not a dormitory. It is a small apartment consisting of a living room, a kitchen, a bathroom, and a bedroom.

6 September 1990

I still have not heard from transportation regarding my shipment from home. If I don't think about it maybe it will come. This day was a nice day. It was so nice to have children speak when they enter the room and when they leave. We had a grade level meeting today and found out that there are so many activities available to us.

I went to the bank to withdraw the interest on my savings because I was running short of money and was quite disappointed at the low interest accumulated. I was told that Korean banks pay 14 percent interest.

I often feel that being here is just a dream and that I will wake up and find myself back in Virginia. I think about Gerald. I have not heard from him since August 3rd, although I have written to him several times. I hope things are going well with him. He is considering taking a job in California. I would prefer he didn't go so far, but I have left the decision up to him. I pray daily for him and hope that he will be guided in the right direction and that no harm will come to him. I've told him and Tavia that life is a struggle, but there are some joys. We must take the bitter with the sweet and learn from our mistakes, trials, and tribulations. Things will work out for them. I will continue to help as long as I can. My mother and father helped me as long as they could, far into adulthood.

7 September 1990

Friday is the end of two full weeks of work. Thank Heaven, everything has gone along fine. I have to keep *tight reins* on my class. This afternoon, for those who had done all of their assignments for the week, I gave them free time or play time. They are allowed to bring in table top games to play with their classmates.

After work, I went to the hairdresser. From there I went to the high school to meet with a travel agent, Lorna Skye. Sam, Katie and Kathy were already there. We made plans to travel to Bangkok, Singapore and Hong Kong during our Christmas break. The winter break here is longer than in the States. When we leave school on December 21st, we won't return until January 6th.

There are many opportunities to make extra money. I applied to teach calligraphy, as an extra-curriculum activity. Also, I read that there is a need for people to transport adopted babies to the States.

As I stated before, we get daily American television programming, so I know about Klan demonstrations in Washington, blacks moving back south and the continuing saga of Marion Barry.

I thought about Gerald's going to California. I told him the choice was his. One never knows what is for him until he tries it. Experience is the best teacher. If things don't work out, he can always come home.

I watch *The Today Show* every morning and Arsenio Hall Show each night. The things that are happening in the world and the Middle East affect us all. We need to become more concerned about each other.

Every morning between 6:15 and 6:30, drill/exercise teams jog past my street chanting as they go and carrying a flag. They are members of military companies. They often hold up traffic, but they are fun to see.

8 September 1990

I have Tia's picture hanging on my bedroom mirror. I think of her often. She loves to go walking, play on the playground, and go to the library. I am waiting to hear what the doctor says about her speech. I am considering sending Tavia money to take her to a speech pathologist. We will monitor her step by step.

The day was a lovely day for me. I began with my usual morning reading and meditation. I then went to Moyer Recreation Center where the bus was to leave to take us on a tour of Suwon City and the Yongji Temple. There were two couples, two tour trainees, the tour guide and me. One of the Korean tour trainees was on the boat ride with me last week. She was glad to see me. I took a picture of her and she asked if I had the film developed yet. I hadn't. The two couples were of mixed race. The two American men had been married to the Korean women for over thirty years and had lived in Korea almost forty years.

Our first stop was at the walled city of Suwon. A magnificent wall surrounded the entire city. It was much like the Great Wall of China. In the wall were holes for cannons and at the top of the hill was a large stone structure which served as a torch to communicate with other communities. It was interesting that while we were there we saw military persons and large groups of school children walking about the grounds picking up trash.

From there we went to a lake and amusement park for a picnic lunch. After eating, I walked around and a Korean restaurant owner beckoned to me to come. When Koreans want you to come to them, they appear to be waving good-bye. When I went in, he turned the fan toward me and poured me a cup of water. He watched TV and occasionally glanced at me as I sat at the table. I pretended to sip the water because we were warned not to drink water while off base. He asked me how old I was and when I told him he laughed and shook his head. I walked farther and stopped in a restaurant where Korean women were on the floor cleaning seafood. Koreans eat all kinds of seafood. I have tasted squid. It is okay. We noticed a slanted roof with water running continuously over it. This was done to cool the inside of the building.

We left the amusement park and went to a Buddhist Temple. The monks were there and were very friendly. Before entering a Buddhist temple, one must remove his shoes.

As we left, there were high school students playing a game. One approached me and wanted to borrow my sunglasses for the game. He returned shortly, bowed and thanked me and asked to take my picture with one of the students.

There was also a very colorful group of military men who wanted me to photograph them. By then I had run out of film. I was quite disappointed. The traffic was very heavy coming back.

We passed several grave yards. The Koreans bury their dead on the hillside in mounds.

I returned home, grabbed a quick bite, changed my clothes and went to South Post Chapel for an unaccompanying person Christian fellowship. A young man gave a Bible presentation of one of the beatitudes. Afterwards we prayed. Another gentleman took out his guitar and we sang Christian songs.

9 September 1990

It started raining last night and rained hard throughout the night and early morning. It even thundered. It did stop, however, about 10 a.m. to allow me to get to church and back without getting drenched. As I forestated, when it rains here it pours *rivers* of water.

I attended Gospel Service at Memorial Chapel and just as last Sunday the service was uplifting. Chaplain Mangey's topic was *Frightening Facts for Fickle Folks*.

After service I stopped at the public library to schedule a visit by my class on Monday, September 17th. I also registered for and received a library card. From there I went to Moyer Recreation Center to weigh myself. I was down one pound from last week. I am now in the 19th hour of my weekly 24- hour fast.

I left Main Post and returned to South Post where I live. I stopped by Dragon Hill Lodge to purchase the Sunday paper, buy some won and a loaf of bread. I found out that I couldn't purchase won at the lodge since I was not a guest. I took my newspaper to the lounge area and began to read. It was difficult because three Korean men and a young lady were in the area talking. When they sensed that they were annoying me they apologized and moved to another area.

The Korean term that I learned for this week is "shille hamnida" which means "excuse me."

It was really funny watching some of the Korean TV programs which featured shows like *The Cosby Show*. They had the actors speaking Korean. Imagine Bill Cosby speaking Korean. I learn from and enjoy Korean television even if I can't understand the language, particularly the commercials, the concerts, the dances and the landscape. They, too, have game shows.

10 September 1990

It started raining shortly after I arrived at work. It rained heavily until after 5 p.m.
Today was a very interesting and rewarding one for me. I have spent the entire day in a database workshop. I am finally learning how to use a computer. We will have a follow-up workshop in April. I have two computers in my classroom.
I have a Master's Degree plus 27.5 additional credits. I need 2.5 more credits to get a raise on the Master's +30 salary scale. I hope to get the additional credits by December when I will finish the Study for Teacher Training sessions.

11 September 1990

It rained all through the night. I was thinking with all the talent, ability and money in our family, if only we could have been closer, no one would be suffering now. I hope that we will grow closer to try to meet each other's needs. I see Ada, my sister, and Joyce, her daughter, as hurting very much. They need to be closer. Marian says she has not heard from the family since Mama's death. Marian is suffering in a quiet way. She is very strong and takes life one day at a time.

Afternoon: 11 September 1990

It is still raining. It has been raining heavily for over 24 hours. The children came to school for a half day. The high school had to close one and a half hours early. Roads were blocked because of the flooding from the River Han that had swollen. Workers were sent home early and teachers were stranded. People who had lived in Korea for fifteen years or longer said that they had not witnessed such a downpour since they have been here.

I have finally gotten a new neighbor. The apartment across from me has been vacant since I've been here. The young lady who moved in is a new teacher at our school. We talked, then my other neighbor who is president of our Women's Support Group came down to tell me that the meeting was canceled due to the rain. I asked for a candle should the lights go out.

I don't regret not bringing my car. The traffic is just like Washington, D.C. and Northern Virginia at rush hour. They say Seoul has more accidents than any other city in the world.

12 September 1990

I woke up with the weather on my mind. We were told to watch TV and to listen to the radio for school closings. I hadn't heard anything by 6:30 a.m., so I called Kathy and she said DODDS were closed. I, in turn, called Tammy to tell her. There was flooding everywhere. Some buses couldn't get children home until late.

I did my usual morning reading, became bored and decided to go out to shop. As I was leaving, my cleaning and laundry lady Mrs. Whan, came in. She is the nicest person. She made beds, but I made my own. She washed dishes, cleaned the house and laundered my clothes. It is a good feeling leaving for work looking good every morning.

On the way down the hall, I met Paula. She was coming to check on me. We chatted a little. The lady who presented fashions at the retreat and her daughter had to stay with Paula because they couldn't get home due to the rain.

When I got downstairs, I ran into another teacher who said she had just gotten a call to come to work. So I went back upstairs, got my things and went to school for the workshops that we didn't finish on Tuesday. After that we went over to the high school to hear Dr. Blawn speak. Dr. Blawn was over all DODDS in the Pacific region which included Japan and the Philippines. He spoke to us about the state of DODDS since many servicemen were being sent back home. He said Korean schools were quite stable for the next four or five years. Teachers raised questions about not being able to get transfers to other regions. There was concern about certification and why the schools were closed since it had stopped raining by 9 p.m. last night. It was quite an informative meeting.

I found out that I will not be taking part in the Study for Teachers Training because I have had the training under another name in Virginia. It was called *Skillful Teacher*. I knew that, but I thought I could get away with taking it again. I would get seven days off from work and three graduate credits.

After leaving the meeting I went over to Main Post to get a few things done. I got some pictures out and put in some more film. I then went to pick up my business cards and shoes I had made. I wear size 8 ½ Korean size. I was advised to wear them for one month before having the cobbler make me another pair. I stopped past the Army Community Service to renew my loan of household items since my things had not arrived. I went home to eat and then went to the commissary to shop. The weather was still dry.

I called home at 7 p.m. I called to wish Gerald a "Happy Birthday," but Tavia said he wasn't in. She said the television was on in his room, but he wasn't there. She said he usually turns things off before he leaves. I thought perhaps he had gone out to his car.

Gerald called me back and I was glad to hear his voice. He said he had been so busy working two jobs that he hadn't found time to write. He was steadily preparing to go to California and it seems as though he is making progress. I pray that this is the break he has been looking for.

Tavia said that the doctor told her that as long as Tia is talking to some people and not others there is no need for a speech therapist. I didn't agree with this totally. She still needs monitoring and her speech should be diagnosed by a speech specialist. I will feel better about her situation when I hear from an expert.

13 September 1990

Weather-wise, this was a lovely day. Things went well. My pay stub was not in my mailbox but that was no indication that my check hadn't reached the bank. At 1 p.m., Fred Proctor's dad came to deliver Fred's birthday ice cream cake. It came from Baskin Robbins. He came barging in the door with his buddy and told me I looked tired. I was. We had been meeting to the extreme. Mr. Proctor forgot a knife to cut the cake so he went across the street to Burger King and came back with two plastic knives. It was a struggle to cut the stiff ice cream cake. We sang "Happy Birthday" to Fred and I had him and some of the other children help to serve the cake. It was delicious.

The knob of my front door came off. Also, my clock was found on the desk minus the batteries so I had to rely on the children to keep me on target as far as time. After school, I had to attend a meeting that lasted an hour. We got out of the meeting at 3:40, too late to go to the bank to check on my pay since the bank closes at 3:30 on payday.

After arriving home, I changed my clothes and decided to walk up to Dragon Hill Lodge since the day was so nice.

I returned home, made a salad and heated up the beefaroni I made the day before.

Several Koreans were killed in Tuesday's flooding and many lost all they had.

14 September 1990

The day went well. At least it was a dry day. I usually allow the children to have 25 minutes of free time on Friday afternoons, but they were rather talkative so I took their playtime away. I don't think they minded since they had the ice cream cake party yesterday. After school I went to my school mailbox and found a note from one of the teachers inviting me to dinner on Saturday evening, but because of the tour I opted for brunch on Sunday.

I then went to my other mailbox to get my pay stub. I had direct bank deposit. I was disappointed with my pay because health insurance had been taken out and a payment for the advance pay that I received. So I had to cut back on my bill payments and the money I wanted to send to Tavia and Gerald. Besides, I had to make a payment to the I.R.S. I had to cash a bond. Thank God I had that to rely on.

I went to the bank and the post office to get some won (Korean money). I stopped by the PX to buy some film. They were rearranging the store which made shopping inconvenient. There was a basket sale at the Moyer Recreation Center. I am not a basket person but I went anyway. I found a flat basket which could serve as a tray or to be hung on the wall.

A flyer was also in my box asking for donations of food and clothing for the flood victims. I have a few blouses that I will donate.

I am enjoying my stay in Korea but work is no picnic. We have to work hard. I bring work home every night which I didn't do in the States.

15 September 1990

The day was a great day. Forty-five members of the school staff went on an all day tour which cost 10,000 won ($14.00). Everyone was on time except the principal and her husband. Nat, the trip coordinator, said that he would leave them, but he wanted to eat next week.

We went first to the Tourist Information Center where a spokesman told us about the history of Korea, showed us a film, allowed us to tour the facilities, served us Ginseng tea and gave us a poster and a gift packet on Korea. The spokesman said he had been up last night until 2 a.m. at a party and hoped he could remember everything correctly.

From there, we went to Changdoh Palace - Puvon (Secret Garden) where the last king of Korea lived and died. He was the 27th king. Mr. Kim Win, our guide, is a 14th generation Korean. He is quite handsome. He informed us that the Japanese invaded and occupied Korea from 1910 to 1945. He also told us that the king wanted to marry a Japanese princess, but her doctor told her that she could not bear a child. So the Japanese princess married a prince. After marrying the prince, she conceived and bore a son. After that, the doctor was killed because of his false prognosis.

Our next stop was Camp Mount O - Pines. This is where I will take my class for our outdoor education program. It has lodges, a campfire area, volleyball nets, hiking grounds, etc. We had a delicious spaghetti lunch there.

We traveled on to Bugak Skyway Drive which took us to the top of a mountain overlooking Seoul. It was on tightly secured military ground, so we couldn't take pictures until we got to the top and only of the countryside, not the city of Seoul.

In the souvenir shop, I purchased a fan. On the way home we stopped on a street where vendors were. There, I purchased pairs of men's socks, a plant, chopsticks, a change purse and a small cowry shell circular mat.

I packed the socks and purse in a box to send to Alston

Street Baptist Church along with four other small gifts for the senior citizens of Pendleton House. They had given me the money before I left the States to make the purchases.

16 September 1990

Although it is Sunday I got up at 6 a.m. I did my usual personal reading and did some schoolwork which included reading, checking papers and cutting out and pasting pictures. Just before taking my shower, the telephone rang. It was Selena Wilks calling to see if I was going to church. Of course I was, so she said she would pick me up at 10:45. After taking my shower, I called Edna Edwards to find out if she and I were still going to have brunch after morning service. We were. I got dressed and went downstairs to wait for Selena. She was a little late. I talked a little while to Mary Canty, a fifth grade teacher, who lived downstairs. She was sweeping and picking up beer cans from yesterday's cook-out and party. She informed me that they had fun and that I should have come. I wanted to say to her that I wasn't invited to come. But instead I told her that I was exhausted from yesterday's tour.

Selena came and we drove on to church. The service was great as usual. Chaplain Mangey's topic was *Heaven: The Christian's Home of Record.*

After service Edna and I went to the Main Post Club for a champagne brunch. I had never been in this building before. It was nice. They even had a casino. There was food and there was food. I ate and I ate. Reverend Mangey and other members came in later.

The invitation to have brunch with Edna was a blessing. I told her about my mask presentation and my school note cards. She was ecstatic. She showed me how she could promote them and get me engagements. She had been in DODDS for twenty-five years and she knew everybody and everything. We would work as a team to put the program together. I looked forward to big things here in Korea. I now needed Jenny to send my looseleaf of my mask presentation, the videos that were made of me in the States and the masks from Ned and I would be on a roll. I went over to the school to take snapshots of the school so that I could sketch it and present a portfolio to Mrs. Knoy, the principal.

17 September 1990

We had an assembly first thing. It was Citizenship Day and it was also in conjunction with Constitution Week, September 17-21. The day went along fine. The knob of my door came off for the third time. I had another teacher take it to the repairman for me.

I ended my weekly 24-hour fast at 2:30 p.m.

I was thinking of the day we went to get the things from Mama's apartment. Everything was so neat and in order. I believe she spent most of her last days making sure that everything would be just right. No one knew how much she suffered. She wanted it all to end.

Tavia is doing the best that she can to keep everything at home okay. I hope to send her some money to go to Angie's wedding in March.

About 7 o'clock, Edna Edwards came over. Together we planned strategies for setting up my *Role of Masks in African Culture* presentation. I am now waiting for my looseleaf and my hold baggage so I can present a complete portfolio to the principal for approval.

18 September 1990

When I got to work, my door wouldn't open. Since the knob fell off yesterday, the custodian locked the door with his key. He later informed me that maintenance people would make the adjustment.

We had another meeting after school. We have been having meetings two and three times a week.

I learned that I was elected as a teacher representative to the Teacher Education Association of Korea. Representatives will meet in Taegon on Saturday, but I have a Korean conversation lesson then. They will travel to Taegon by train. I hear that the train is indeed a luxury ride.

19 September 1990

The class walked to Yongsan Library which was on Main Post. The library is as large and as complete as any large city public library. There are 134,000 books and 50,000 pieces of other material. After that we returned to the school to go to art class. From there the children went to the school library to borrow books. They then returned to the class to take an hour long spelling test. They worked up until lunch time, then returned to class to complete the test. The test was part of what is called *compacting*. If a child scored high, he could go into a sixth grade book. We didn't have time for any other subject except social studies. I was giving a social studies test the next day and I needed to prepare the class for it.

We held *Open House*. It was from 3:15 to 3:45. It is the one day in my teaching career that I hate. This day went well, however. There were about twenty parents.

I came home first, and had chunky chicken noodle soup and a very delicious sweet tasting Korean cracker for dinner.

I also went to my second Korean conversation class. My teacher is young and full of energy.

20 September 1990

When I got to work, I found my application for funding for the Study for Teacher Training Class in my mailbox. It had to be typed by noon. Ms. Ridgely, the assistant principal, told me that one of the secretaries would do it. I later got a call from the office stating that Ms. Ridgely had no authority to tell the secretary to type it for me. I didn't think she had as much authority as she claimed to have had. I did get the math resource teacher, Nat Nalls, to do it. He was a jack of all trades. Ms. Ridgely was the one who told me I couldn't take the course, but I got the okay from the superintendent.

I am still having trouble with the door knob on the door of my classroom.

It is very interesting to look at the Korean women's shoes. They are very, very pretty. The women have small feet so many styes are available to them.

I went to Main Post and I noticed the riot squad was there. Evidently, they suspected some unrest or demonstration. The members of the riot squad looked like teenagers.

I attended Phi Delta Kappa's dinner and slide presentation on Korea at Dragon Hill Lodge. The dinner was superb and the slides great. Phi Delta Kappa is a professional education organization.

21 September 1990

The telephone rang at about 5 a.m. It was Gerald. I was glad to hear from him. It seemed that everything was moving along smoothly for him as he prepared to leave for Alameda, California to take on a new job with the U.S. Department of Agriculture. I believe he will do just fine. He has always been industrious and willing to learn.

The fifth grade classes went to Seoul Grand Park Zoo, all two hundred students. The zoo has every and just about all types of animals in the animal world. When we got off the bus, we took a train car to the zoo. I had five parents to accompany us.

When I returned to school I found out that my application to teach calligraphy has been accepted. I will teach calligraphy to the children for a total of 20-39 hours.

Gerald called again to give me the address and phone number of the hotel where he will be staying.

22 September 1990

Today I took my first train ride. We went to Taegon which was a three-hour ride. Marcia Cain, who lives downstairs, and I were supposed to go to the train station together, but she knocked on my door about 7:10 a.m. clad in her nightgown. She had overslept. She brought some fruit because we were to have breakfast on the train. She had already called me a cab, so I took my ticket from her and was on my way. I went to the Seoul Station where I met with the other teachers. We boarded the train and were somewhat disappointed. It was not as luxurious as we were told. Later, I found out that it was not one of the luxury lines. It was nice, though. The velvet chairs could be turned to face each other and that is what we did. Each chair also had a tray which came in handy. Shortly after boarding the train, the teachers started pulling out plates and bags of food. We had quiche, orange juice with champagne, blueberry orange nut muffins, fruit and M&M's. We arrived in Taegon three hours later and took a cab to Camp Henry for our meeting at the school.

There were teachers there from all over Korea, which included Puson, Taegon, Osan and Seoul. Ella Mead, whom I had met in Kansas City, Missouri, served as secretary of the Teacher Education Association of Korea. After the meeting we went over to Camp Walker for a catered picnic of chicken, baked beans, potato salad, rolls, ice tea, and lemonade.

We were reimbursed our expenses at the meeting. I was glad of that. Some of the members had planned to stay overnight. Four of us returned to Seoul. While I was in the train station, which was extremely crowded, I was in awe. It seemed as if I was dreaming and at any moment I would wake up and find myself back in Virginia. The ride back was nice. I took the subway back to the base and walked from the base gate to my BOQ. It was about 10:15 p.m.

23 September 1990

It is Sunday and I decided to go to South Post Chapel for service. It is a quieter Baptist service but I like it. I missed the bell choir because I was a few minutes late. There was a guest speaker, Chaplain Joseph Mills, who served at Fort Leavenworth. After service, Paula Riff came rushing out. I didn't think that she ever missed a service at Gospel Service. She said the service wasn't emotional enough for her. She was the one who spoke on single women at the retreat. In the church bulletin there was a tear-off request for prayer. I tore it off and wrote a prayer request for Gerald as he relocated to California to take on a new job. I also ran into a teacher from Seoul International School whom I met on Thursday at the slide presentation dinner. As usual I couldn't remember her name. I gave her my business card.

After service I walked to Dragon Hill Lodge to try to get my refund check cashed and to buy a newspaper. I couldn't cash the check, so I purchased the newspaper and sat in the lobby to read it. As I headed for home I ran into Mary, my neighbor, who told me I could get my check cashed at the Main Post Exchange. The hotel clerk told me the same. Mary told me she received her hold baggage last week and hers was shipped from the states on August 15th. Mine had not arrived. She urged me to check daily. She said that one person went to the movement office and found her things just setting there.

I stopped at Moyer Recreation Center to see the photo exhibit and the silkscreen print exhibit done by my co-worker.

Once at home, I prepared a dinner of salisbury steak, macaroni, a salad, applesauce and crackers. I finished grading papers when Mary came over and brought me a sweater should I get chilly. It is near the end of September and it is becoming chilly.

I talked to Selena today. She was highly upset because her BOQ was so crowded. She said she couldn't get to the bathroom nor could she sleep in her bed. She had a four-bedroom house in North Carolina and shipped just about everything over here to a one bedroom apartment. She had her two bedroom sets shipped, three televisions, dining room set, etc.

24 September 1990

It was on this date fifteen years ago that Daddy passed away. The memories are still fresh.

Gerald is traveling by Amtrak to California. I associate Amtrak with derailment, but I pray for Gerald's welfare, place prayer requests at both post chapels and ask friends to pray for him and I believe this is the opportunity that he has been waiting for.

The day went well. I had the class to write servicemen aboard the U.S.S. Fairfax. A couple of the students said that fifth grade was boring. For some, they could play all day, watch movies all day, party all day and they would still say life was boring.

25 September 1990

I attended an all-day teacher training session. I went to school first because the training did not begin until 9:00. It was a good thing that I did. My substitute had not shown up. I sent Ben to the office to inquire at what time my substitute would be coming. The secretary, Jan, sent a note stating that if the substitute didn't show up by 9 o'clock, she would call for another. At 8:55 the assistant principal, Warren Pike, came to fill in until a substitute arrived. I arrived at the meeting late, of course. The District Superintendent of Schools was there. I had taken this training before in Virginia but not for credit.

I checked my mailbox and found mail from Gerald. It was the address of his new job in California and the pictures I took of Mama at rest. I looked at them and thought of her. The way she was prepared did not resemble her at all.

This page begins another journal book. A great idea struck me. Why not make my journal into a book. With Jenny's help we can write it. No one I know of has written a book of life in DODDS. We read and see movies about servicemen, but not the teachers who serve the children of servicemen.

After the training session, I rode with Marcia Cain to the filling station to get gas. This ride took me to a different section of the base. She suggested that I take the post bus and just take a round trip of the base to find out where places are located. She also informed me that she had adopted a black/Asian teenager who is 13 years old (black father/Korean mother). She lives in a BOQ like mine which is extremely crowded. She just received 4,000 pounds of household goods from the States. Keep in mind that we only have a kitchen, bedroom, living room and bathroom. She does not need a teenager sharing a room with her. Teenagers need some privacy and space.

26 September 1990

This was the second day of the all day seminar on Study of Teacher Training. It was very good and well presented. For lunch, we went to the Main Post Club for a buffet.

I stopped by my classroom to check things out. My substitute left a note saying she didn't know that she had to accompany the children to the library and that the librarian was upset. How foolish! Anyone knows that children have to be supervised at all times at school.

I was somewhat relieved when I heard a pediatrician on TV say that by three years old a child should be speaking well enough to be understood by others. Tia still has some time. She is so bright otherwise.

27 September 1990

If Gerald left for California on Sunday I should have heard from him. Sometimes no news is good news.

The day went well. The children had health screening which included weight and height measurements, hearing and eye checks and a check for scoliosis. Scoliosis is a condition that can be detected early. It affects the spinal cord causing a curvature in the spinal cord.

I went to pick up my Korean han-bok (dress). Mrs. Park, the dressmaker, had only the top and the slip. Originally the slip that cost an extra 10,000 won wasn't included. Since I had no idea when I would wear the dress after I leave Korea I decided if I got tired of the skirt, I can have it made into a dress. The total cost for all the pieces was 100,000 won or $130.00. Several teachers had the dress made so we would wear it at school when we celebrate what the Koreans call *Chusok*. This year Chusok falls on October 3rd. It is a time when many Koreans travel to the mountains to offer food to their deceased ancestors. Since many would be out of town on the 3rd, we decided to celebrate at school on Friday,

September 28th. The parents would bring in all kinds of Korean foods.

I will begin teaching calligraphy on October 15th, so I stopped at the library to pick up some books on calligraphy.

28 September 1990

This was the day that the school celebrated Chusok, the biggest of the Korean holidays. It's like our Thanksgiving, Memorial Day and Christmas combined because they cook a big feast and travel to the mountains to commemorate their deceased ancestors.

Food started "pouring" into the classroom at the beginning of the day. Some parents came at our regular lunch time, but I told them to come back at 1 o'clock. The mix-up was that the flyer that went home said to have the food at the school by 11:15 a.m.

I changed into my han-bok at lunch time. Only one child dressed in her Korean clothes. After lunch I read a story to the class as usual and we had a math lesson. After that the fun began. While the parents heated the food and prepared to serve, I led the class in a discussion of the Chusok celebration.

I asked Sara An, Nicolas, Wayne and T.J. to fill us in on how they celebrate Chusok. I added my knowledge of Chusok. Then I had a parent to read an article written by one of our culture teachers and published in the school's weekly newsletter. I then had each child who brought in food to describe it. There was kim bap (sushi-raw seafood), kimchi, yahi mein, cucumbers, fried rice, a Korean dessert, chocolate cake, nachos, cookies, shrimp chips, punch and other foods. I put the cake in the school refrigerator to serve on Monday.

One parent brought a video camera and other parents and I took snapshots. It was a great successful day!

After school, all of the teachers who were dressed in Korean attire took a group picture on the campus.

After school I went to the bank. The line there was wrapped around the building because the bank would not be open on Saturday. The lines moved quickly, however, and I returned home, ate and then went off to Korean conversation class. I am beginning to make progress in class. Needless to say I was pooped, but I had to make one last stop and that was at the shoppette where I picked up a few food items

I was warned not to go to the commissary because it would be crowded with Koreans buying all kinds of food, particularly fruit for Chusok.

29 September 1990

I awakened with my Korean conversation class on my mind. I did my usual morning reading and then studied the Korean alphabet. I was glad that I did because it helped out in class. One of my students and her parents were in this Saturday's class. I am registered in the Saturday class, but I sat in on the Wednesday and Friday classes.

I returned home to do some schoolwork and to fix lunch. I was interrupted by a knock at the door. It was a Korean man trying to get me to subscribe to the Korean Times. I did. It cost 1200 won for six days. They don't deliver on Monday. Twelve hundred won was about $1.55/$1.60. He shook my hand and bowed about six times before he left. I asked him how to say *newspaper* in Korean. He said words which were about a sentence long. I told him to forget it. He wanted to know what nationality I was, how long I would be in Korea, and if I had a husband. Quite nosy, I would say.

The teacher of this morning's Korean speaking class, Mr. Cho, attended T.C. Williams High School in Alexandria. He said he lived near Memco in Annandale. He and I talked about several places in Virginia. He too, wanted to know what nationality I am. He said I speak differently.

This evening I went to an unaccompanied personnel fellowship at South Post Chapel. This was my second visit there. They served chili, crackers, cookies, pretzels, chips and soda. I can always find food! The young leader spoke to us from St. Matthew 5:9 *The Beatitudes* (blessed are the peacemakers). He then asked for prayer requests, so I asked him to pray for Gerald and he did. I haven't heard from Gerald, but somehow I believe he is doing fine. He has just been busy settling in.

At the fellowship, we sat around and talked. I found out that the leader lived in Woodbridge. Another couple had been stationed at Fort Belvoir and their two children attend my school here in Korea.

30 September 1990

Today, the last day of the month is a nice one. I did my usual reading and some schoolwork. I am now in my 24th hour of weekly fasting.

Selena called me about 9:45 to find out if I was going to church. I had planned to go to South Post Chapel because I didn't want to walk to Main Post, but I changed my mind after Selena called. She said she would pick me up at 10:55, but it was after 11:00 when she arrived. She said she couldn't find her keys. The last time she told me she would pick me up at 10:45, but it was 11:00 when she showed up.

Of course service had already begun. There was a guest singing group from Maui, Hawaii. They were very good. I snapped two of their pictures on the way out of the church. Although the group, *Straight,* was billed as a sermon in song, Reverend Mangey preached anyway.

Selena and I hung around church to see who we could see. Then we went over to the PX. After that, Selena dropped me off at Moyer Recreation Center where I had signed up for a dry brush painting on bisque glass. The class was to last from 2:00 to 4:00 p.m. We made a Halloween pumpkin man. I was very pleased with it and I plan to send it to Tia.

1 October 1990

This was a big week for the Koreans. They were celebrating Cho-suk on the 3rd and also Foundation Day. Some were taking off the entire week and traveling to the mountains.

I forgot to mention that Saturday night I woke up about 1 a.m. with thoughts of Mama on my mind. She died in June of 1990. I thought about her last days and how I wished I could have seen her before the morticians took her body away. Jenny told me of how she embraced Mama after she took her last breath. I wish I could have been there to do the same. She told me of how she watched as the morticians prepared Mama's body to leave the house to be taken to the funeral home. I recall that the woman lying in the casket had little resemblance to Mama and so the funeral service was not so sad to me.

I was pleased to receive my box of note cards from Tavia today. I was also pleased to hear that my hold baggage was in Seoul, but it will not be delivered to me until next Tuesday afternoon between 1:00 and 5:00. It was consoling to know that it had finally arrived. I had been wearing the same clothes over and over and the weather was becoming chilly.

We had a nice day at work. I served the cake that was left over from Friday.

I have not heard from Gerald. It has been a week now since he was to have left for California. I assume that he has become so busy that he has not had time to write. I hope that no news is good news.

I went over to Edna's BOQ. Edna has been in the DODDS program for twenty-five years and has been in Korea ten years. She needed some help with a course we are taking. She was also concerned about two courses she needed to take to be recertified.

2 October 1990

It was two months ago that I left the States heading for Korea. I was so fortunate and blessed to have this opportunity to come. I am still enjoying my tour. I have been received very well.

I received a letter and a book of spiritual poems from Ada, my sister. She is now going to school but she did not say which courses she is taking. I also heard from Allison Smith, a very dear friend who was also a deaconess at Alston Street Baptist Church. She is a very sincere person. I cherish her friendship very much.

I also received campaign literature from Jim Moran, Mayor of Alexandria, who is running for state senate. Included also in my mailbox was an absentee ballot.

The day went well. We viewed a one-hour long video on sharks.

After school, I attended a meeting on extracurricular activities. I will be teaching calligraphy.

This evening I went to the Women's Support Group meeting. It was interesting. As I mentioned, the emphasis was on *Know Yourself, Know Someone Else*. We were given an assignment to record and examine our emotions. We had a gathering of sixteen women.

When I got home, I stretched out on the sofa, fell asleep and the next thing I knew the alarm was sounding. It was 5 a.m.!

3 October 1990

Many places are closed today because of Cho-suk, and many of the Army post places are staffed by Koreans. The bank, the commissary, the recreation center, and several other places were closed.

I put in for leave for October 9th to be at home when my boxes arrive. We were given a day off for this. It is referred to as *moving day*.

As I was walking to my building, Rene' Ennis called to me. She was the teacher whom I said lived off Frye Road. She said she lived near Frye Road. Guess where she lived? In the same block that I lived in. She lived at 4257 Buckman Road. She lived in Alma Robins's building in Alexandria. The way she found out was that Alma wrote her and told her that Daisy Goodwin was teaching in Korea.

I met with the faculty representatives to count ballots regarding the days we would have for parent-teacher conferences. The staff seemed to favor Wednesday afternoon and all day Thursday and Friday. This means that I would have 2 ½ days off for conferencing, three days for my Study of Teacher Training workshop and two days off for Thanksgiving.

4 October 1990

This was a "light" day as far as teaching goes. At 8:15 a.m. military policemen came to give a presentation on D.A.R.E. (Drug

Abuse Resistance Education). At 9:40 the children went to Korean culture class until 10:20. At 10:30 they went to the media center for a lesson on reference skills. At 11:40 they went to lunch. At 12:35, they watched *Square One,* a math show on TV. I did manage to get in some reading, handwriting, math and social studies.

When I arrived home, I prepared dinner and did some schoolwork. Afterwards, I began diligently studying my Korean conversation lesson, when the telephone rang. It was my Korean instructor, Mrs. Campio, calling to inform me that class was canceled for the night. We usually meet on Wednesday, but since the day before was Chosuk it was moved to tonight.

The days are becoming shorter and the weather cooler. I look forward to receiving my hold baggage on Tuesday. I need some warm clothes.

I received a call from Tavia. I was just thinking about her. This was indeed mental telepathy at work. I was so glad to hear from her and to hear that things are going well. I was almost floored when she told me that Gerald drove to California, he had gotten there safely. Indeed the Lord was with him. I had to stop and praise God. I had everyone praying for him and our prayers were being answered.

I informed everyone in the States that if they wanted to send me a gift for Christmas, make it money so I can have money to spend on my trip to the Far East.

5 October 1990

It is Friday, Thank God!!! I should not complain. I like it here. We are not pressured and I don't have to work so hard. For instance, today after our opening exercise, the children watched *Reading Rainbow* on TV for a half hour. I then taught reading and I began a five unit spelling test. I had to stop because at 9:40 the class went to physical education class. When we returned to class, the reading teacher came in to talk about a reading incentive class. After she left, I continued the spelling bee until it was time for lunch. After lunch there was English, math and social studies. After school Dora Johns stopped in to find out if I would be interested in going on a field trip with her class. Of course my answer was in the affirmative. In our conversation she mentioned that the officers' wives would have a bazaar in November. I showed her my note cards that I market and she said that I could sell them there.

I gave the winners of the class spelling bee a pack of note cards. Here again this was prospecting and advertising. Some children said their parents would probably buy some.

I received a call late at night from Amy Smart, the president of the Teacher Education Association of Korea. She asked if I would serve as M.I.P. (Minority Involvement Personnel).

6 October 1990

The day was a nice one. I arose, did my usual morning reading and some schoolwork. I then went to Korean conversation class which lasted past 11:30 to after 12 noon. I left there and went to Main Post to withdraw some money from the bank. In Saturday's class, the instructor put sentence after sentence on the board and phrase after phrase and taught us how to read them. I didn't remember them nor what they meant. I could, however, read Korean.

I returned home and did more schoolwork. Kathy called to ask me if I would join her for a salad at the Golf Club, but I had rolled up my hair in preparation to go to the dance. I proceeded to take a nap since the dance would last until 2 a.m. and I usually go to bed quite early.

I was awakened by a knock at the door. It was Paula Riff wanting to borrow ice because she was defrosting her refrigerator.

Selena called to tell me that she would pick me up at 9:30. At 9:30 I was downstairs waiting. As usual, no Selena. I went back upstairs to use the hall phone to call her, she was just combing her hair. She arrived later and said her clock was slow.

She noticed the note cards that I had on display on the table and took two packs. When we arrived at Eighth Army Club for the Kappa Alpha Psi Scholarship Dance, there were several people there and plenty of food. The tickets cost $10.00. The dress was to be casual. The folks had on everything from casual to way out. There was a guy there with a SILK suit on. Three dancers who looked like they were from *Soul Train* took over the stage and dance floor constantly. They were good, though. They looked like "rappers" which reminded me that there would be a rap contest the next week.

I saw a fellow I had met earlier and he told me to save him, a dance. Another fellow at the table asked me to dance and I told him, "Not now." I found out that if you turn a fellow down the first time he wouldn't ask you again. I sat for quite a while before I got to dance.

I found out at the dance that our music teacher taught at Silverbrook Elementary School in Fairfax. I met another lady who taught in Reston.

Half the Gospel Service church members were there dancing and having a good time. Even Paula Riff, who was the president of Women's Support Group was there. I didn't know what she was drinking, but she had a glass. Since no one asked her to dance, she went over and grabbed a guy, pulled him up on the floor and was holding on to him as if he was going to get away. Soon afterwards, I saw her on the floor with a different fellow holding him just as tightly. Selena was the popular one. She was asked to dance several times and I saw her give a fellow one of her business cards. We decided to leave at about 11:30 p.m. because the crowd was thinning out. This was the latest I had ever been out.

7 October 1990

The caterpillars have gone and now there are large flying creatures that look like dragonflies. They fly away from people -

Thank God - and they stay outside.

I awakened at 7 a.m., did my usual reading, had breakfast, wrote Ned and did a pencil drawing of the school which I hope to make into a note card and present to the principal for marketing in the school store. I called Selena about 9:15 to let her know I was going to church. She was asleep. I then took my shower and got dressed. She picked me up on time!!!

This was Communion Sunday. Reverend Mangy spoke from Acts 4th chapter and Revelations 21st chapter. The dance crowd from last night was there. The mother of my student, Fred Proctor, was also in attendance at church. I had just written a note to Fred's parents because he had fallen asleep twice in one week while the librarian was teaching and while I was teaching. He said he had gone to bed at 10 p.m. His parents requested a conference. I will meet with them within the week. My neighbor was at church. He is a very handsome, slightly grey haired gentleman. Selena asked me why I hadn't "checked him out."

Selena and I mingled awhile after service. We then went to Seoul Friendship Arcade. She was going to buy a chest. I looked at a three-tiered one that I would like to have.

I returned home, finished sketching the school, read the newspaper and took a nap.

When I awakened about 5:35 p.m., I called Edna Edwards to tell her I was coming over so that we could go over our home assignment for the Study of Teacher Training course. We spent about two hours gossiping. We then got to our homework and reviewed it for about 30-40 minutes, if that long. Then it was back to gossip. She had some miniature fruit drinks that one could buy in the Korean grocery stores. They were very tasty. They came 5 to a pack for 500 won, which was about 75 cents. She offered me some grapes and tea but since I was in my weekly 24-hour fast, I declined. I took the drinks home. I did, however, drink a glass of lemon/lime water. She also gave me some *Caress* soap which is good for dry skin. My face is very oily, but the rest of my body is dry. She also told me that if I squirted some baby oil in my bath water along with my bubble bath, that would alleviate dryness.

She said rubbing oil on my skin after my bath would help also. I stayed there until about 9:45. Edna's building is a few yards away from mine. Despite the safe environment of the base, I still didn't like to be out at night alone. So I ran the few yards to my BOQ.

8 October 1990

Schools were closed today in observance of Columbus Day. I awakened about 6:45 a.m., read and inked in my pencil sketch of the school. At 8 a.m., I broke my fast and had cold cereal and coffee for breakfast. A knock came at the door. It was Paula Riff. She was defrosting her refrigerator and wanted to put some of her food in my box. I think she just wanted to see what I had in my refrigerator. A little later, Mrs. Hwan, my housekeeper came in to clean.

At 1 o'clock, I attended the Yongson Christian Community Festival at South Post Chapel. It was great. Colonel Will Franklin, the Chief-in-Command of the entire base was there with his wife. I took their picture. I sat behind some of the top Korean officers, such as Admiral Ha, General Hivang and several others. I shook hands with them and took their picture. Major Michael Long, a member, was one of the speakers. He looked just like Kenneth, my nephew.

A Korean choir sang and the choir from Gospel Chapel sang. The Gospel Choir sang an old song a capella. It was quite appropriate. Then both choirs sang together. One song was performed with hand motions. The sermon was delivered by a Baptist Korean minister.

Afterwards, there was a lovely reception. Young Korean men and women dressed in native clothes sang Christian music accompanied by brass instruments, guitars and violins. They really had the western spirit. There were all kinds of Korean and American foods. All the top military brass was there.

9 October 1990

I was excited about this day. It was the day I was supposed to receive my hold baggage from the States. I arranged to have a half day off since delivery was promised between 1 and 5 p.m. When I arrived at school the transportation office had called on Friday and again on Monday to confirm that the delivery would be made. With that thought tucked away, I spent the before-school time reproducing the sketch of the school that I made. During my break, I was able to duplicate two sizes to assimilate the way the cards would look. They were beautiful if I may say so myself.

The substitute showed up about 10:50. I proceeded with my lesson, then gave her instructions before leaving. She told me that this was her first time substituting.

I left class, went to the main office to look for Mrs. Knoy, the principal. With my note cards in hand, I finally caught up with her outside of the lunchroom. She was elated with the card replicas and told me how talented I am. She said she would pass the cards on to Pat Gonza who is in charge of the school store where the note cards will be marketed.

I left there to go home and wait for my hold baggage to come. I busied myself by checking papers and writing lessons for the calligraphy club. I also watched Donahue whose topic was *peeping toms*. There was also a feature on Jermaine Jackson.

I waited and at approximately 3:45 my hold baggage came. There was a person from customs and another from transportation. My girlfriend said that no one from customs came when her freight was delivered. Maybe they just made spot checks. He wrote the serial number of my keyboard. There were several things damaged, which included my two African masks. One was broken in several pieces, my picture was broken, half of my china and a casserole dish. My three hats were bashed flat and my clothes were badly wrinkled.

I spent some time putting things away and then I took a break and went to Dragon Hill.

I returned home, ate and put away the rest of my things.

Paula Riff stopped by earlier to get her food from the freezer. She looked all around. She was quite nosy.

10 October 1990

This week is Fire Prevention Week. In keeping with the observance, I took my class to the fire station across the street from the school. The fire chief demonstrated to the students how to get out of a burning house. He allowed students to go through the demonstration and they enjoyed it. Afterwards, he allowed the class to take a ride around the base in a decorated fire truck. I went along. It was fun. The children, I should say, Henry Carn clanged the bell as we rode. Upon our return I took pictures of the class and several of the Korean firemen posed for me. They got a kick out of being photographed.

I checked my mailbox and my pay stub and a package from Tavia were there. The cost of postage is quite expensive. My pay check is still not as I expected. I went to the Army Community Services to file a claim on my damaged property when I ran into a co-worker and neighbor who told me that the men making the delivery dropped the box containing my hold baggage and she would serve as a witness if needed.

I then went to Dragon Hill. From there I went to Korean conversation class, but the teacher didn't show up. One of the staff called her and she rescheduled the class for the next evening.

I had a conference with Fred's mother. She said he had always had problems with reading and if he goes to bed at 8:00 he doesn't go to sleep so she let him stay up until 10 p.m. She said she was disappointed that he lied to her about doing his homework.

11 October 1990

I just can't get it together this morning. I didn't like what I laid out to wear and so I have to change my clothes. My plans are to go to the NEO (Noncombatant Evacuation Operation) point to register in case of an emergency. Well, I arrived at work later than usual and found out when I got to the door that I had forgotten the key to my classroom. Luckily, I live across the street from the school. I was able to register anyway. I was glad I did because as the day wore on the line grew longer. I was glad, too, that I changed my clothing because I got several compliments on what I was wearing.

I was in my room eating when Katie Zinns stopped by to say that she heard I was good at calligraphy and that a colonel was looking for someone to print name cards for guests at a ball in November. This was an opportunity for me to make some extra money. This also gave me an opportunity to show and tell her about my note cards. I gave her two of my business cards - one for her and one for the colonel.

As I was going to Main Post crossing the busy Korean street, I got that feeling again that I would wake up and find myself in Virginia, but that was eight months away. Time was ticking by, though.

I went to the bus terminal to wait for the post bus to carry me to the commissary to do my marketing. I came home, grabbed a bite to eat, then off to Korean conversation class. Ms. Campio apologized and explained that she had to go to a tea with her husband yesterday, family first and volunteer work second.

12 October 1990

Today is the official Columbus Day. We didn't discuss it at work because about four weeks prior we had social studies lessons on Columbus and his landing in North America. I had a full size picture of Columbus which I divided into 4 parts by drawing a line down the middle and across the center. I assigned a part to each child to draw. On Monday, I stapled the parts together to make whole pictures.

After work I went to the Family Care Center in Dragon Hill Lodge. I got the works, a pedicure, a manicure and my hair done with color.

I am still working on my apartment. It is beginning to look even better. I receive a lot of compliments.

13 October 1990

It is Saturday. I read as usual and hung some beads on my living room drapes. My place is looking better. I had cold cereal and coffee for breakfast then off to Korean conversation class only to find that the classroom door was locked and Mr. Cho, my instructor, was waiting in the vestibule lounge area. This gave him a chance to ask me more questions. He had to leave to go to get the key. Meanwhile, the other students came in and we chatted. As a part of this session, Mr. Cho filled us in on some Korean customs.

I came back to my BOQ, heated some soup and had crackers and grapefruit juice for lunch. By that time I had to go to Main Post for a lecture on Korean architecture.

While on Main Post, I got an estimate on my school note cards. Another thought grabbed me to have the sketch made up as prints to market. I also signed up for a tour of Syngman Rhee Memorial and the National Cemetery on Sunday.

There was to be a Gospel Extravaganza at Memorial Chapel. I called around to try to get someone to go with me, but had no luck. As the evening wore on, I didn't want to go anyway, I decided to stay home, go through my papers and practice playing my keyboard.

14 October 1990

I awakened at 6:30 a.m. and read. I finished reading a chapter I had to read for the Study for Teacher Training course and did the quiz at the end of the chapter. I skipped breakfast because I was in my fasting period and opted to play my keyboard. I enjoy entertaining myself and I am amazed at the number of songs I can play. Since it was early in the morning I kept the volume down.

After practicing, I read my morning newspaper, when the phone rang. It was Tavia. I was elated to hear from her and hear that all was well at home. She was debating over a job offer she had received. I encouraged her to take it. I told her some factors to consider in making the change; the location which is in Virginia, traveling against the traffic, meeting new people, and the possibility for promotion. I told her that when one makes a move, he always loses something but often one has to lose in order to gain. Tavia is a hard working, industrious and conscientious daughter and is very faithful to her work. Her skills are such that they can be appreciated by anyone. She has helped others to accomplish at the expense of being hindered herself. It is time that she was rewarded for her accomplishments. I believe if one doesn't feel that he's being treated justly, don't stop being the best you can be, keep doing your best for eventually someone will see your good. Persevere and in time you will find your place in life. That is the way Providence works. I say, " Go for it."

I attended South Post Chapel and I heard later that I missed a dynamic service at Gospel Service at Memorial Chapel. Edna told me that Reverend Mangey preached well, the male chorus sang for the first time and the Masonic Order worshiped in the service. Some Masons ushered.

I returned home, practiced my keyboard some more, then went to Main Post to catch the tour bus to Dr. Syngman Rhee's mansion and the National Cemetery. Syngman Rhee is considered the founder of modern Korea. His mansion appeared small in comparison to western standards. Houses of common people surrounded his. He was good at calligraphy, so I purchased a copy of his manuscript in calligraphy. I also purchased a cylinder shaped pencil holder.

From there we were taken to the National Cemetery. We saw the large mound and shrine where President Syngman Rhee is buried. There was a large delegation (2 bus loads) of Japanese visiting the cemetery. On the grounds was a section where the generals and flag officers were buried in mounds. One gravestone read 1930-1962. This was a person who was a general at age 32.

On the ground was also the actual hearse with the body of President Park inside in a glass encasement. We could see the flag draped casket through a window. The hearse was intact as it was in the funeral in 1979. There was also a museum housing photographs of patriotism. There were many pictures of the Japanese invasion of Korea and the Korean war. One of the fellows on the tour was amazed that I knew so much about Korea. Believe you me when I leave here in June, I will be an authority on Korean culture. I even had an opportunity to use some Korean words while on my tour.

We arrived back on Post a little before 5 p.m. I returned home and began to prepare a meal since my fasting was almost over.

Edna Edwards called and later came over. Shortly after she arrived, Selena and Leo dropped by. We exchanged conversation for awhile. After they left I ate a meal of chili, salad, crackers and coffee followed by a glass of Chablis. I was exhausted from all the walking, so I stretched out on the sofa.

15 October 1990

This has been a day! I had about a half dozen people come to my room during the day to interrupt my teaching. It began with Chloe McMichael who came in with my doorknob in her hand and a message to send my new students to the counselor at 9 a.m. Then others throughout the day. I made it through, though.

I received a package of mail from Tavia and a letter. She had already told me over the phone Sunday what was in the letter.

My class was extremely noisy and weren't very conscientious at all. I stayed at school a little later than usual.

I came home, ate and then went to the Army Services Community Building to file a claim for my broken items. As for the government, they take you through many changes. I was given about five forms to fill out, besides I had to call an inspector to come out to inspect my items.

16 October 1990

I'm not sure whether the alarm went off or not but I didn't awaken until 6:15 a.m. I got to school by contract time which was 7:40 a.m. Today went nicely. The children were happy that their homework was easy.

After work I went over to Main Post. I had signed up for an Oriental floral arranging class, but I was just too tired. I stopped by Moyer Activities Center to tell the instructor that I couldn't make it. I was the only one who had signed up anyway. I stopped by the shoe maker's to pick up my shoes, but when he couldn't find them, he noted that the day he promised me was Thursday. I had Tuesday on my mind for some reason. Walking had scuffed my heels and I was having them spruced up. I then stopped to look into a course that Troy University was offering. It was just what I needed for my program in the States. There were two sessions being offered. I opted for the one where you meet on three weekends, Saturday and Sunday. The course cost almost $600.00. I was hoping to get some reimbursement from the school system.

I waited for Major Malett to come. He was the person whom I talked to about doing calligraphy on the place cards for the Marine Ball at the Hilton Hotel. I needed to go back to school because I noticed my door to the classroom was unlocked and I also needed to mail the friendly letters that I taught my class to write. I didn't want to leave my BOQ because I might miss Major Malett. But as luck would have it, he called to say he was bathing his children so he would come around 7 p.m. At that, I went to school, checked the door which was locked, mailed the letters and stopped at Burger King to get a diet Coke. Major Malett was late because he couldn't find my building. He was a typical all-American type guy. He had on a jogging suit. He said he lived in Woodbridge and was stationed at Quantico. He was pleased with my calligraphy, but had to present it and the cost to the board on Tuesday. He asked me to print a sample so he could take it with him. So I cut two pieces of paper the size he wanted and printed two names in two different styles. The military is quite demanding. I thought this may lead to something else. He also asked that I come to the hotel should additional people come as I would need to make them place cards.

17 October 1990

I had taken the morning off because the claims inspector was coming at 9 a.m. to inspect the broken items from my hold baggage. He was prompt. I showed him the damage and he made note and asked me to stop by his office next week to get a copy of his report to take to the claims office. He said it usually takes a week to ten days to receive a refund. I spent the next half of an hour practicing on my keyboard. I left for work at 10:30 a.m. although I wasn't due there until eleven.

I found the class in the library. The afternoon was filled with interruptions including the lock repairman. I received a note from the principal asking me to meet with her regarding my class' conduct in the lunchroom. I had to delay the meeting because of my calligraphy club meeting. The first session went well. More children signed up than I expected.

18 October 1990

Today was about as hectic as yesterday. The M.P. from D.A.R.E. (Drug Abuse Resistance Education) came to talk to the class. We then watched *Square One*, a math video and then there was an assembly which was scheduled for 1 - 2 p.m. It only lasted until 1:30 p.m., so I took the class back to the room grumbling. They wanted to play on the playground until 2 p.m. Keith Turner and Jeremy Skelt didn't return to the class. I tried to reach them at home. Jeremy's brother said that Jeremy was outside playing.

After work I went to Main Post to check on a flight to the States, and to get some library books for my course.

I went home, ate, read the paper, wrote two letters, wrote an article for the newspaper and this journal.

19 October 1990

Jenny called to tell me that she had to get $250.00 work done on the car. She was complaining. I considered that little since Jenny would be using my car for a year. The government would have paid for me to keep it in storage. I was never so depressed as I was when I got those two phone calls this week from Tavia complaining and telling me about Gerald and Jenny complaining.

20 October 1990

I thrust myself into my work to forget about last night's phone calls. I took my note cards to school and put them on the table in the lounge. I didn't get any sales by the end of the day, so I took them home. Selena paid me, making my total sales $57.00.

I gave Marcia Carn a write-up on me and a snapshot for the school newspaper. I worked religiously and finished my report cards, displayed some things in my room and wrote my assignment for my second calligraphy class.

After work Selena came to my room and we went to the bank on Main Post, came back to South Post to find out if we could join the exclusive Hartell House. Hartell House is an exclusive private club and a very fine place to dine. We then went to Bentley's in the Dragon Hill Lodge for *Happy Hour*. We both ordered strawberry daiquiris. They served veggies and a dip, potato salad, roast beef and rolls. Berry and Flowers joined us at our table.

21 October 1990

I awoke about 6:30 a.m., still depressed over the phone call I received from Tavia asking for money because her car had gone bad. Heaven, Help! I got up and read from Titus, St. John 14th chapter and Philippians 4th chapter to gain strength to make it through the night. Everything seemed to be crashing in on me.

As I reflect back over my life, I think of from where I have come. Starting out in the poor section of Baltimore, working my way up through trials, tribulations, joys and sorrow to where I am, halfway around the world. But not once did I waiver from my belief in God and my belief in myself. Despite all, I have tried to do good to all, although it may not have been perceived as such. I have always believed that God has been molding me and shaping me for a good cause. I thought of Mama and Daddy, how they gave what they could. I thought of Gerald and Tavia, the fact that I could not always give them what I wanted to give them, but I gave them what I could under the circumstances. I guess that is why I help them so much now, and constantly think and am concerned about their welfare. I feel that somehow I haven't given them all that they need in life. I write and write to them more now and talk to them to encourage and give guidance and hope. I think about the next few years and the direction they will take me. I will just depend on Providence to guide me.

22 October 1990

I went to the first class of my three-weekend course. I had to give a report. I tried hard to focus in on the lesson and I managed. Class was dismissed about 45 minutes early so I went to the library to do the next day's assignment.

I walked home, ate, lined 22 more place cards. I needed an outlet, so I went to Dragon Hill Lodge.

I returned home, had a glass of lemon water, inked in the place cards and called Edna Edwards. Edna teaches at my school. I prayed to God that I wouldn't get a depressing call today. Misery has a way of following you everywhere, but God is everywhere, and I am comforted.

The telephone rang at about 10:40 p.m. I was very jittery. I knew it was from the States because no one here calls me so late. It was Tavia. She said that she had reached Gerald at work and he sounded fine. He also said a co-worker was going to help him find a place to stay. I thanked God for answering my prayers.

23 October 1990

I am in my fifth hour of my weekly fasting. This is the second day of my weekend class in Psychological Foundations of Education. We were dismissed again 45 minutes early which meant I didn't get a chance to give my second report.

As I was leaving the Post I saw Flowers, a fellow I met at *Happy Hour*. We chatted briefly. I continued to walk to South Post when one of the students in the class I am taking caught up with me and we walked and chatted. He lives not far from me.

I took a nap, woke up at 11 p.m., worked on the Marine Ball name cards and did some of my college course work and went back to bed about 12:30 a.m.

24 October 1990

This morning it is raining hard. It hadn't rained here in weeks. The day went well. Pat Gonza gave the class an introductory lesson in computer use.

I met with my calligraphy club for the third time. We practiced forming lower case letters and practiced writing brief messages on note cards. The children did a fine job.

I went home totally exhausted at 5:57 p.m. I thought I'd take a nap. It worked well last night.

I awoke at 9:30 p.m. and read some of my course material and watched Arsenio Hall.

25 October 1990

It became very dark and started to rain with thunder. The children were hyperactive, which made the day crazy. They screamed when it thundered, but believe you me they didn't do it again. I allowed them to use the computers today to put in data.

I called the hospital to make an appointment with internal

medicine to get a prescription for my medication. My appointment is for next Tuesday at 3 p.m. I will go to the 121st Hospital for Family Practice. Dr. Smit is the physician. We are assigned a physician by the last four digits of our social security number.

When I got home I called the claims office to check on my money. They said a voucher would be sent to finance and I should get a check next week which would not cover the cost of my big mask. I am waiting for a receipt from Ned to be reimbursed for the cost of the mask.

The assistant principal returned my report cards after checking them and she said they were great. Amy Smart, president of T.E.AK., stopped by my room to ask if I would be interested in attending an education conference in Delaware. I was indeed.

I had two pupils who were in special programs for slow learners. The programs didn't seem to be helping, so I set up a program of my own in the classroom.

26 October 1990

This was a half day for the children. School was dismissed at 11 a.m., so we only had time for reading, library and spelling. At my lunch break, I stopped at my mailbox and was surprised to see a letter from Sean, my nephew.

I went to the store for some junk food, then returned to work to read from my course textbook. I then went home and erased the lines from the name cards I had printed the night before.

27 October 1990

The phone rang. It was Selena inviting me to a birthday party at the Embassy Club. When we arrived everybody and his mother was there. I asked how everybody knew about the party and I didn't. Come to find out the honoree, Lee Frank, was a member of the bowling team and Selena and I were not. Even the superintendent and his wife were there. There was food and there was food. Selena and I were the only minorities there and then in came Paula Riff. I had been drinking a beer because I wasn't going to pay for a mixed drink. Since Paula was president of our Women's Support Group at Gospel Service. I thought I would respect her, so I hid my beer can behind my chair. Guess what, Paula came in, went straight to the beer barrel, took out a can of Lite, flipped the lid like a pro and turned up the can. We lingered on a little while, then left about 8 o'clock.

28 October 1990

Thank goodness for small daily pleasantries that keep my spirits high. I am ever so grateful for my art talent. I am highly admired for it.

My class wrote to the sailors aboard the U.S.S. Fairfax which was deployed in the Mediterrean Sea.

A bright moment in my day was when a Korean mother brought me a bouquet of a dozen roses. It just made my day. I later went to the photo shop to pick up my snapshots and they turned out lovely.

29 October 1990

Today the staff went to a Korean restaurant. The temperature has really dropped. It is cold. We rode through Seoul to the Dae Wou Gak restaurant which was formerly a ginchi house. (A house where Korean women pamper men). There is still one large such house left in Korea. It cost about 200,000 won a night which is about $280.00 in American money. The restaurant has several traditional huts on the grounds which typify the traditional Korean lifestyle. We toured each, then went to the main house for dinner. We had to leave our shoes outside. We entered, sat on the floor on cushions at very low tables. Then the waitress started waitress started bringing in the food. There was a salad, raw vegetables such as carrots and cucumbers, soup, tea, kimchi," squid, rice and beef which was cooked at the table. We ate the food with chopsticks. The soup and rice we ate with a large spoon. We took the beef, put it in a leaf of lettuce, rolled it and ate it. For dessert we had sliced apple/pear, a cross of the two fruits.

After dinner, there was a live dance show. Five types of dancers were presented. They were beautiful. There was the sword dance, the monk dance, the shaman dance and two others. The musicians were super. I took pictures. It was a delightful evening. We departed for home.

Major Malett called, then stopped by to leave an up-dated list of guests for the Marine Ball.

30 October 1990

Night before last I went to bed very tense, fearing that I would get another bad phone call from home. I feel the same way tonight.

I awoke this morning and read a chapter from my course text book. I then prepared to go to Moyer Recreation Center. One of my students was there with his mother selling his toys. Other children and their parents came by and there were several teachers.

31 October 1990

The weather has become quite cold. I went outside to catch a cab. There was none, so I boarded the post bus which is free. Everyone else had the same idea of boarding the bus because the bus was crowded.

I went to the beauty salon which is located in Dragon Hill Lodge. It too, was crowded. I got there at 4:15 and did not leave until 7 o'clock. When I arrived home, the telephone rang. My heart skipped a beat because I knew it was from the States. It wasn't a bad call after all. It was Tavia calling.

1 November 1990

I got up, read a chapter from my Study of Teacher Training course and printed 20 more name cards. I decided to go to South Post Chapel for Protestant service. There was a guest speaker whose delivery wasn't the best, but his message was great. He talked about letting the *Lighthouse*, God, lead you through the fog and storms of life no matter what kind of sailing vessel you are. I saw several faculty members there. Three of them had Korean children with them whom they had adopted. Henry Carn, my student, was there. He was showing me his new blue jacket which had an eagle on the back.

I left church, went home and fixed a meal. I finished reading a chapter for my Psychology of the Foundation of Learning course, then went to Main Post for a two-hour course in ceramics.

I made and decorated two vases. One was a marbling design and the other was a splattering one. The instructor told me he would fire them and I could pick them up on Tuesday. There are several other people who are making ceramics. One female sergeant made several lovely pieces, in fact two shelves full. The slip only cost $3.65. Use of molds is free, but each firing costs a quarter. I can't wait to get mine.

2 November 1990

I set the clock for 5 a.m. but I didn't get up when the alarm went off. I laid there, fell asleep and woke up at 6:15. I had to get dressed and eat a quick breakfast because Edna and I would leave for Main Post and Memorial Chapel at 7:20 a.m. We stopped to get some film. The Chaplain announced on Sunday that the buses going to Lotte World would leave at exactly 8 a.m. When we arrived the sponsor announced that buses would leave at 9 o'clock. We had one good bus and three dilapidated army buses. One bus had all teenagers and were they acting up. Lotte world is the equivalent of Disneyland and Disney World in the United States.

We arrived at the Lotte World Adventure Land about 9:45.

When the teenagers got off the bus, they started clapping and singing. The Koreans were looking at them and thought they were demonstrating. The teenagers' behavior was disgraceful.

After that, the day went lovely. Edna and I walked through a department store merely to get away from the teenagers

When we entered the park, there were musicians lined up and all the characters that you would see at Disneyland. I took a picture with one of the characters. We walked around and decided to go through a tunnel by boat through the adventures of Sinbad. It was scary and fun. We also rode the monorail. The roller coaster was frightening, so was The Conquistador, which is a swinging boat.

In mid afternoon, there was a parade of the characters and floats representing a dozen or more countries. They danced and played instruments. It was so exciting. I wished Tia could have been here. We then walked around and had lunch. Next, there was a stage show of acrobats and other performers. They were outstanding. It was Disney World Korean style.

When we got ready to go, we found out that one of the buses had broken down, so we had three to accommodate us all. There was room enough because two of the four buses were half filled. And guess who was on our bus? You got it. The rowdy teenagers! Sons and daughters of the righteous church leaders. Besides that, there was a guy who appeared to be in his 50's sitting behind us popping gum. Heaven, help!

After arriving back at base, we went to Morning Calm, a self-help center for home repairs. I picked up light bulbs, plastic and two switch covers. You can get what you need there and you don't have to pay, which makes sense. We were using the hardware on the residences on the base.

3 November 1990

Edna gave me some ginseng tea which is very popular in Korea. Koreans say it will keep you well, sane, happy, etc.

Today is my sister, Peggy's, birthday. I sent her a gift and a card.

The thought just crossed my mind that there is still some goodness and joy in the world. I believe that if we continue to seek it, we'll find it. We have to put our priorities in order. Life should not be filled with the purchasing of material things all the time. It just keeps us in debt and we become so depressed. One should spend money on spiritual joy and environmental happiness. There are things that people can do to be happy, rather than buy to be happy. I am content with what I have, and I'm happy with what I do.

4 November 1990

Today the children were better behaved.

After work I went to the 121 Hospital. I was running out of medication and I needed a prescription filled, so I made an appointment with internal medicine. Each visit cost $67.00! The doctor checked me and gave a prescription for the medication. I asked for some vitamins too. My appointment was at 3 p.m. I arrived at 2:25 p.m. The doctor saw me at 4 p.m. I had to wait at the prescription counter so it was about 5 p.m. when I left.

I rushed home and changed my clothes to go to a cocktail party that the three principals at my school were giving for the teachers. It began at 6:30 p.m. It was nice. The buffet consisted of the usual, quiche, sheabah, sausages, chicken wings, deviled eggs, sushi, beer, wine, and punch.

While at the cocktail party, I talked to Rene Ennis. She said she had heard from Alma, my former neighbor in the States today. Rene was bored and wanted to return to the States. She spent her time working, shopping and partying. I was hoping to find out what Korea has to offer and learn to enjoy the culture.

I stayed until about 7:45 p.m. I needed to get home to work on the Marine Ball name cards. I had about 100 more to do.

5 November 1990

I received a letter from Jenny today filling me in on everything. I also received my package of mail from Tavia and a letter. Ada Donstan, a missionary friend, wrote too. She informed me that Dottie Seals and Mrs. Lucinda Taylor passed. Mrs. Seals was a missionary and a custodian at Grace Baptist Church. Mrs. Taylor was a missionary to Africa. Ada Donstan was still complaining about the missionaries. She made reference to the people who had left the missionary society and the church. There seems to be much friction there still at the church.

I took a nap at about 8 p.m., woke up at 12:30 a.m., printed 20 more cards, wrote in my journal and tried to get some more sleep.

6 November 1990

Today is election day in the States. I mailed my absentee ballot a couple of weeks ago.

I spent all day today in a workshop. Before I went to work, I printed 20 more Marine Ball place cards.

I went home for lunch and erased the pencil lines on the place cards.

We were dismissed at 4 o'clock so I stopped at my classroom to prepare for the next day. I then went to Main Post to Moyer Activity Center to glaze the two vases I made on Sunday. I got a ride over with Tony, a fellow I met when I first arrived in Korea. I took a bus back home, prepared dinner and began work on the second set of Marine Ball place cards.

I had just begun when Selena knocked on the door. She hasn't seen my apartment since my household goods came and she was surprised that I had embellished it so.

She and I planned how we would spend the rest of the week. Right after she left, Edna stopped by. Poor Edna. She has such little confidence in herself. I wonder what she did before I arrived in Korea. I lent her my notes again and she was grateful.

An hour later, Major Malett came by with the final list of names to be printed for the Marine Ball. The total list is 410. He said the fellows had decided to pay me a little more money.

7 November 1990

I arose and printed about 22 more name cards for the Marine Ball.

I went to my classroom to check on the class and to give the substitute some last minute instructions. I then went to Yongsan South Post Chapel for my training.

It went well. After the training there was a memorial service for the logistics director for the schools of Korea who had died of cancer. He was in his 60's.

8 November 1990

I went to the beauty salon today to get a relaxer and a manicure. After arriving home, I changed clothes and waited for Selena. She came promptly. We went to Itaewon to shop where I purchased a purse, a tam, and some Christmas cards.

I returned home very tired. Major Malett called to say that he would come to bring the last of the names to be printed. So far I have printed over 300 name cards.

9 November 1990

I had to attend the third day of Teacher Training. I did however, go to my classroom to get the class started and to see if the substitute needed any help. The training session was over at 1 p.m.

Major Malett called to say he would stop by to finalize the name card project I was doing. I told him to come about 8 p.m. because I had to go out.

10 November 1990

I called Selena and Edna to invite them to my Korean conversation class commencement. Neither was at home, so I went alone. I then called Selena and Edna again. I did reach Edna and she attended the commencement. It was very nice. The table was spread with chicken, cheese and crackers, deviled eggs, cookies, finger sandwiches and candy. There was also a large cake made in the shape of a basket with "Congratulations" written on it. There were several people there including my university instructor, Dr. Swalt.

There was a short ceremony at which time I received certificates. I took pictures with my instructors and classmates who hadn't brought their cameras. We all received a little book called *Face to Face* which contrasts Korean and American customs.

11 November 1990

Today is Veteran's Day. When I got up this morning, I did my usual Bible reading, then read one of my three newspapers which had started to pile up, then read most of the next chapter for my Psychology of Foundation of Education course. I then went out to the post office to send off my journal pages and a tote bag for Tia and one for Tavia

I was able to find a pair of low heel black shoes and some Christmas cards. I then went to Main Post to cash the check I received from Major Malett for printing the place cards. I also signed up for a tour of East Gate Market and South Gate Market. These markets are unusually large. You may see a building with nothing but shoes. Another that has only blouses.

I rushed home and changed my clothes to go to *Back Home Hour*. *Back Home Hour* is a time when all the black gospel singing groups (15 in all) come together in a gospel extravaganza. It was beautiful. One guy who was on crutches, threw down his crutches and shouted all over the place. I took many pictures. After the program, dinner was served.

I rushed home to change clothes to go to a fraternity dinner, fashion show and dance. Awards were also given. The sister of one of my school children won first prize, a $300.00 savings bond. The dance was lively. The Omega officers wore purple tuxedos, purple bow ties and gold shirts, their colors. They had a beautiful display of plaques, pictures, their mascot (a bulldog), etc. They also had an ice carving. The Omega Phi brothers raised a toast and later joined hands and sang the Omega song. At the dance, a few guys were doing some kind of stomp dance accompanied by dog/wolf noises.

I met two fellows, one I had seen before. I was not really interested in either. But if I wanted male companionship, they would do.

12 November 1990

I got up at 9 o'clock and read from my psychology book. I was becoming hungry so I went to Dragon Hill Lodge to eat. I ordered two enchiladas with slaw. Each meal was served with tacos and a dip.

I came back home and prepared to go to Main Post for the Eighth Army Band Concert. Before I left I read some more. While I was on Main Post, I purchased a scrapbook for my snapshots. I then picked up my pieces of ceramics. They were lovely. I took a picture with my instructor. The concert was in the same building where the arts and crafts were made. The music was very soothing. I wouldn't suggest that anyone go if he was tired. He would fall asleep.

13 November 1990

Tony Nix, a short fellow with a closely shaven head called me. I met him at the Omega Dance. I don't know why I gave him my telephone number. I watched him afterward. He seemed to be a playboy.

14 November 1990

I had a very busy day. It rained just about all day long. I was so glad that our fall book order came. I sent it off on October 4th. The children were becoming anxious. I also received my package of mail from Tavia. She said Tia's speech was getting better. I praised God for that as I pray for her daily. I believe she is going to do fine because she is a very bright child. I sent her some books from school, a tote bag from Lotte World, a card with my picture and some other pictures. I also sent Stanley, my brother, a snack pack of Korean junk food. I think about him and pray for him daily.

I also received a letter from Sean, my nephew, who was doing super! He sent me a copy of the first copy of the school newspaper of which he is assistant editor. I was so proud. Our family has talent. We just have to keep channeling it to benefit us. Tavia, my daughter, is skillful in supervision; Jenny, my sister, in math; Jennifer, my niece, in architecture; Gerald, my son, in marketing and science; Kenneth, my nephew, in several areas; and Joyce, my niece in education. I hope we can pool our skills so that we can live a comfortable life.

15 November 1990

I held my fourth calligraphy club meeting today. Afterwards I stayed at work until 5:30 p.m. I would have never done that at Overview School in the States. I praise God everyday for this opportunity to be here. I am working hard, but I am enjoying every moment of it.

I was concerned because I had not received requested funds for my transportation to the States. I wrote Amy Smart, the president of the Teachers Education Association of Korea, hoping she would intercede. I knew that things would work out. I just had to have faith.

16 November 1990

The morning was a very chilly one. The day went well. I met with Warren Pike, our assistant principal, who reviewed my certificate for DODDS.

I was anxious yesterday because I did not receive my advance pay from OEA (Overseas Education Association) for my trip to the States. But thank God it came today, so I went immediately to the airline office to purchase my ticket.

I had a conference with Virginia's parent who was experiencing a number of problems. He didn't get his rank, his father was suffering from cancer and his wife had to work until 8 p.m. at night and his daughter was suffering. He felt that the school wasn't fulfilling his daughter's needs. He was not happy with the TAG (Talented and Gifted) program his daughter was in and he thought the class wasn't lively enough for his daughter. "Your daughter needs to be lively," I told him. She didn't interact with the other children at all.

So much for that. I agreed to counsel with his daughter, Virginia, and get back to him the next afternoon.

17 November 1990

I dropped off a box of used clothes for underprivileged Koreans at South Post Chapel. Oral Roberts says, "When in need, plant a seed," which means when you are depressed and suffering take your mind off yourself and do something for someone else. So that is what I did.

Edna stopped by my room because we were supposed to have a pre-conference for our observation in conjunction with the course we were taking. I left my material at home so she and I went to my apartment to have our pre-conference. She had her tape recorder since she couldn't take notes. Heaven knows how she made it through college. She was rather slow and admitted it.

I stopped at the school office earlier to pick up a letter which would authorize me membership at Hartell House.

18 November 1990

The substitute came so that Edna and I could observe each other teaching. I met with Rosa, the assistant principal, to do a progress report of my class. The children spent most of the afternoon watching a video.

Virginia's father came to another conference with me. I found out that she had a mental block. In my progress report to the principal, I expressed concern for Virginia. The principal suggested that Virginia have counseling. The parents had Virginia at a late age and they were very protective of her. She looked old, homely and old fashioned. I had time to think so I was ready for her father. I think I surprised him. He reminded me of the military parents in Northern Virginia. They seem to think that they can throw their rank around. Some would come to conferences in full regalia, stripes, stars and all. I never knew whether it was to impress teachers or to threaten them. I was never impressed nor threatened. I always addressed them as Mr. or Mrs. I knew nor recognized any rank. To me they were parents, dads, moms. Virginia's father was too stubborn to give in, but I showed him where I stood in my professionalism and I would not waiver.

19 November 1990

The principal put our *intent* form in our mailboxes. This form is for each staff member to indicate his work plans for next year. I indicated that I would like an art position.

I began to pack for my trip to the States next week. I had faith that it would be a safe and fruitful trip. I will be attending the Minority Leadership Training Conference in Delaware. It will be sponsored by the National Education Association.

20 November 1990

Selena stopped by and we went with Ray to Valerie Winston's house. Valerie was one of the secretaries at the school. She had a lovely home and plenty of food. Valerie's husband was president of Omega Psi Phi Fraternity that hosted the function last Saturday. He was wearing a yellow and purple jogging suit with all kinds of Omega symbols on it. About a dozen *brothers* were there.

I must say the folks over here are living well. They live in very fine homes. We left Valerie's and went to Bernice Thomp's house. Valerie's and Bernice's husbands are majors. Bernice had a lovely bright home. Like Valerie's it too was very spacious.

21 November 1990

As I write my Christmas cards tonight I have a very good and special feeling. I am thankful for the friends that I have met over the years and the fact that we have kept in touch. We have been able to strengthen and support each other through sharing our experiences, the good and the bad.

22 November 1990

This is Thanksgiving day and also the anniversary of President John F. Kennedy's assassination.

I awakened at 7:50 which only gave me time to do my scripture reading because I was invited to Thanksgiving breakfast at Kathy Jannis' at 9 o'clock. The breakfast was lovely. About eight teachers came. It was a light breakfast of blueberry muffins, brownies, peach cake, sticky bread, fruit cup, coffee and juice. We sat around and chatted. I was invited to come along later in the day to Thanksgiving dinner at the dining hall. One has to be invited by a military person in order to eat in the dining hall. Sylvia Carr, a DODDS teacher, was on active reserve and her husband was military, so we went with them. There was so much food and the place was decorated beautifully. It was like a very fine restaurant.

I came home, read part of my newspaper, a chapter from my course textbook and addressed some Christmas cards.

23 November 1990

I awoke and did my usual reading, including a chapter from my course textbook and checked some papers. I then took the post bus to the Main Post to go to the bank to buy money orders for my bills. While I was over there, I picked up film and stopped at the Main Exchange to purchase some pajamas, and a few items for my trip. I returned home, ate lunch then went over to the school to do some work in preparation for next week and the week after. I went home, read the newspaper and played a note or two on my keyboard until Edna came over to work on our course assignment. She arrived at 7:30 p.m. and stayed until 10:30 p.m. By then I was becoming tired and sleepy.

24 November 1990

I awakened at 8:15 a.m. and realized I had to be at Moyer Recreation Center at 9:45 a.m. for a tour of East Gate Market and South Gate Market. I read my scripture and the Daily Word, ate breakfast hurriedly and got to Main Post about 9:50 a.m. Ms. Han, the tour guide whom I had met before, was on the bus. East Gate Market is the largest market in the world. It has buildings of cloth, and buildings of appliances, etc. It was something to see. It was very crowded too. I purchased a wool lined skirt, a miniature gold-plated knife and fork with pearl handles and red Christmas cards. We ate at the Far East Club which was located on a U.S. base. We did a lot of walking. People in Korea push you along, not out of rudeness, but to get by you. Remember, there are about 10 million people in the city of Seoul alone.

I came home, ate something light and read a chapter for the course. Immediately upon finishing, Selena called to find out what I was doing and if anything was happening. I told her there was to be a fashion show at Moyer Recreation Center. Right after she called, Tony Nix called wanting to know if I had an old dress he could wear in a play, then he changed and said it was for an initiation tomorrow. It didn't sound right, so I told him, "No."

Selena and I went to the Moyer Recreation Center in our jeans only to find out it was a dress affair. So we went to the Main Exchange to browse. We ran into several fellows who were at the affair last week including Tony Nix. He had in his hands a lady's black dress and some pantyhose for the *initiation* the next day. I felt sorry for him. I could have given him a dress for the one-time occasion, but I didn't.

25 November 1990

I awoke about 7:15 a.m. which didn't give me much time for a lot of reading. I did read the Bible, my Daily Word and a newspaper. I had two more newspapers to read because I got behind in reading when I was doing the Marine Ball name cards.

I decided to go to South Post Chapel for the Protestant Service. South Post Chapel is just a short distance from my apartment and the service lasted only an hour. The regular chaplain wasn't there, but the service was uplifting anyway. It lasted about 50 minutes. After service I went to Dragon Hill Lodge for an early lunch. Kathy Jannis couldn't join me because she had already had breakfast and she needed to go to Main Post. So I went alone.

I returned home, changed my clothes and went to school to do some planning of lessons for the days I would be away and to plan for my calligraphy club the next day. I also checked my tape for the recording of my lesson for my psychology class.

On the way home, I ran into Amy Smart, driving down the street. Amy is the president of the Teachers Education Association of Korea. She stopped to discuss my trip to Delaware where the Minority Leadership Training Session will take place. She wanted me to bring all the material back that I could because she and I would have to conduct the minority leadership training for Korea. She wished me well on my trip.

I haven't heard from Gerald in weeks although I have written him three times since then. I must continue to have faith that he will be alright. I don't believe that the Lord will take him over 2,000 miles safely and leave him there alone. I believe that God will provide. I prayed constantly for his well-being and for Tavia's, Tia's and the entire family. In the church bulletin, there was a tear off slip for prayer requests, praises and concerns. I tore off the slip and requested prayer for my safe journey to and from the States. I believe this trip is going to be a blessing for me.

As I continued to walk home, Edna drove up in her car. We chatted for awhile. I had a feeling she wanted to meet again to discuss our class assignment, but I had other things to do. I came inside and read another chapter from my textbook.

I ate a light snack and I tried to play a few notes on the keyboard, but I was too tired and sleepy. I didn't sleep well last night. I stayed awake and watched two late movies into the wee hours of the night. I went to sleep about 5 a.m. and woke up about 8:30 a.m. The movie *The Kennedys of Massachusetts* was on. I watched the *Panama Canal* also and learned that over 4,000 blacks lost their lives in building the Panama Canal.

I called Selena. We made plans to meet to go to Hartell House to apply for membership. We had to get a letter from the school to do so. Hartell House is a step above the Embassy Club.

26 November 1990

I got that strange feeling again. The feeling that this was just a dream. The feeling that I would wake up and find myself back in Virginia. I often get this feeling when I am on the streets of Seoul. I have an urge to take a taxi and say, "Take me to 9788 Harvey Circle." It was a very strange feeling, but it lasted only a short period of time, then reality set in.

Today was a disruptive one. It started early on with the children taking a browsing walk through the *Book Fair* to make book selections. Then by 10:50 a.m. the secretary came with a note inviting us to come to see *Maggie, the Clown* at 11:15. Maggies's act consisted of blowing up balloons and shaping them into various characters. She also did a string act. This was the second disorganized assembly we have had. I took my class to the media center and as we entered the room, Rosa, the assistant principal, said for the children to sit in an area that she designated. In the next breath, she said just sit anywhere. My question was, "Do they sit here or do they sit anywhere?" Each pupil was given a balloon to blow up. Then they were told not to blow it up. The teachers were asked to come to the front of the room to get balloons to distribute to their classes. After distributing the balloons, they were given instructions on how to shape a dog from the balloon, few of whom were successful. They were next told to be still and watch the clown do string tricks. The time was ticking away. It was now 11:40 a.m., time for our classes to be at lunch. We were dismissed at 11:45. The children were told that anyone who made a dog out of his balloon to come up front. So they finally got to lunch someway, somehow, sometime. Heaven, help!

As you can imagine, the rest of the day was a wreck. I had to teach the class with their attention divided between the balloon "dogs" on their desks and me.

I held my fifth calligraphy class. We practiced writing italics. We learned how to rule a paper, to space and center letters. The end product was a construction paper t-shirt with Seoul American Elementary School printed on it.

At about 3:20 p.m., Selena stopped by and we went to Hartell House to apply for membership. We were told that we would receive our membership card in the mail in a week.

We left there, and Selena dropped me off at the commissary while she went to get gas. She returned for me about 20 minutes later.

I came home, ate and began to feel so tired. I took a nap at about 5:15 p.m. and woke up at 8:30 p.m. by the ringing of the phone. It was Tony. I told him I was sleepy. So he said he would call back later.

I got up and read a chapter from my course textbook.

I received a letter written on my note card from Elvena of Boston and a neatly written letter from Gerald. I was so glad to hear from him. He informed me that he had found an apartment, but he wasn't fond of the neighborhood at all. He also said that he was adjusting at work, but that he would need a lot of practice to reach perfection. He said the job wasn't difficult. He also told me that he had joined a church.

27 November 1990

My alarm went off at 5 a.m., but I didn't want to get up. I turned the alarm off, went back to sleep and woke up at 6:15 a.m. I read, had breakfast and arrived at school about 7:40 a.m. The day was busy, but not as hectic as Monday. After school, I rode with Pat Gonza to *Toy Alley* to look for some small gifts for my children for Christmas gifts. We walked and walked, but I didn't find what I wanted. I decided to buy pens from the school store through Pat Gonza. The pens were white with a blue clip. The clip has inscribed the school's name on it. We were driven to *Toy Alley* by Mr. Pack, who works in the logistics office. He drove us back by a very quick and easy way, virtually little traffic. I had not been in this area before.

When I arrived home tired, Edna called wanting to come over so that I could help her with her home assignment. I am hoping she won't stay long.

28 November 1990

The alarm went off at 5 a.m. and I got up at 5:15 a.m. The day went well. I had to be in conference after school for an annual review of Audrey Yin's progress. Audrey is one of my students.

I left school and went to Dragon Hill to get my hair done. I got a medium brown color. Upon returning home, I completed my assignment for the Study of Teacher Training course and then took it over to Edna's for her to type. She gave me some last minute tips on going away for which I was so grateful.

When I got home, I received a call from Tavia who told me that Gerald thought I wanted him to pick me up, but I planned to go to Oakland and call him from there. I also received a call from

Selena wishing me a safe trip. Selena is about twelve years my junior.

Speaking of phone calls, there is a telephone in the classroom next to mine. At mid-morning, the teacher next door, Mary Canty, came over to tell me I had a phone call. I get tense when this happens. Who was calling me at work? I got on the phone and the secretary said, "Hold for your call." A gentleman was at the other end. It was Mr. Cho, my Korean conversation teacher, wanting to know if I had developed the picture/film I had taken at the commencement ceremony because he wanted a copy for himself.

29 November 1990

Today I will leave for the States. I arose, read the scriptures and the day's newspaper. I then went to Main Post to get some won from the bank. I went to the post office and to the job to leave my apartment key with Edna Edwards. I stopped pass my classroom to see my children and to let them know I would be gone for a few days. I ran into one of my student's parents at the post office. I guess he wondered why I wasn't at work.

I returned to my apartment, paid my maid and called a cab which was outside my door no sooner than I hung up the phone. The cab driver was quite informative. We talked at length during the half hour drive to the airport. It is easy getting in and out of the airport provided you have all your credentials, which I did. I arrived at Kimpo Airport about two hours ahead of time. Checking into the airport and getting onto the flight was easy.

The flight was almost 11 hours. I left Seoul at about 4 p.m., flew through the night and into daylight in about eight hours. I read most of the time. I couldn't watch the movie *Back to the Future part II* because the sound wasn't working.

I arrived in San Francisco and called Gerald's job to let him know that I was on my way to Oakland and would call from there. I took the shuttle to a hotel in Oakland where I called

Gerald. He came over to the hotel and we had dinner there. We took a cab to his house, met the house lady and talked. We then visited a Mexican gentleman and his family who had befriended Gerald. Gerald was doing well. I was very happy because many people helped him to adjust and to get started. God never fails. We took a cab back to the hotel. I got a shuttle to San Francisco Airport where I met a clown on the shuttle who made a Ninja Turtle from a balloon. I flew to Detroit, then on to Philadelphia.

30 November 1990

I took a shuttle from the Philadelphia airport to the Radisson Hotel in Wilmington, Delaware. My roommate, Beverly Carr from Belgium, had checked in the day before. She was very nice and a strong-minded teacher. She talked constantly of her 9-year-old daughter. She also had a 23-year-old-son. She had been married twice. Later, I took a nap and then she and I went shopping. Afterwards, we stopped at a supper club called "Cavanaugh's." From there we went to the first session of our meeting. There were several people there that I had met before including three of the presenters.

1 December 1990

This was a full day of sessions. I met the other delegates from OEA. Among them was Donald Thomas, one of the Tuskegee flyers of the 84th Division (a group of black flyers that included Coleman Young). I met people who knew people that I knew in the States. I met a fellow from Calvert County who worked with Theresa Morgan who graduated from Coppin College with me. I met a woman, a Native American Indian from Lombardi, North Carolina, who had relatives who lived in the 1300 block of East Baltimore Street in Baltimore.

During the afternoon session, I got a visit from Joyce, Peggy and Ada, members of my family. I was quite surprised, although I did mention in my letter to Ada that it would be nice for them to drive to Delaware. We didn't have much time to spend together, but I cherished every moment. Peggy gave me a monetary gift and Ada gave me a tin of cookies and a Christmas card with a small monetary gift.

That evening the Overseas Delegation went to Sizzler's for dinner. One of the men who was from Germany mentioned that he had one of the old 1943D pennies and that is was worth several dollars. It so happened that I have one. I am in the process of checking its value out.

2 December 1990

We were served continental breakfast this morning just as we were the day before. The morning was spent wrapping up what we had covered. We were seated by states/areas. We talked about what we had to face when we return to our areas and how we would handle our situations in the minority arena. Dean Richards spoke to us about negotiating and empowering. We then heard a report from MAC, the Minority Achievement Committee. This was followed by a Black Caucus meeting which focused on a Black Caucus Conference to be held in South Carolina to address education issues. There was some concern about not getting communications from the Caucus and what the $20.00 membership fee is used for.

We said our good-byes and wished everyone well.

3 December, 1990

Most attendees left right after the conference. I had to stay over until the next morning. I had lunch in the hotel restaurant then went upstairs to find that Tavia, Tia and Tavia's girlfriend, Felicia, had arrived.

I was so glad to see them. Tia had not grown as much as I thought she would have. We went back downstairs and I treated them to lunch. We then walked around the downtown area which was desolate because all stores were closed. We returned to the hotel and they prepared to leave before dark. It was good seeing them again. I spent the rest of the evening in my room relaxing.

4 December, 1990

I awoke early, went downstairs in the hotel and then prepared to board the shuttle to go to the airport. When I got to the airport I found my flight had been canceled due to weather conditions in Detroit. It was later telecast that two Northwest airplanes had brushed wings while taxiing on the runway and had caught fire. One was a DC-9 and the other a 727. Eight people died and fifty were injured. Instead of waiting for the flight the next day, I decided to go to Beth's to spend the day and night and fly out of BWI, Baltimore Washington International. This worked well. I got to talk to Stanley, my brother, a little. I called Tavia and Jenny to let them know I was well.

5 December, 1990

The next morning I awoke about 4 a.m., and left at 5 a.m. to board the 7 a.m. flight to Detroit, and to Seattle, Washington. From there we flew for eleven hours and 39 minutes up the Canadian Coast, over Anchorage, Alaska, the Aleutian Islands over Tokyo, Japan and into Seoul Korea. We started at an initial height of 31,000 feet ascended to 39,000 feet traveling over 5,000 miles to our destination.

6 December 1990

I arrived in Seoul at 7:15 a.m., December 6th. I caught a taxi, called Edna to get my key and then stopped by Paula's to pick up my newspapers. I found out that it snowed while I was away and the electricity was off for a while.

I arrived at school to prepare for the day. I didn't work because I had to attend the Study of Teacher Training workshop.

7 December 1990

This day was also spent in the Study for Teacher Training workshop. On Thursday I received a refund of my county retirement and I was able to pay off a bill. I had to deposit the rest to remain on hold for seven days. I plan to pay off my car by the end of December as part of my goal to return to the States almost debt-free.

8 December 1990

I spent this day in class at The Education Center in the Psychology of Education Class. Today I had to give a report on Marvin Berkowitz, a noted educator. After class I went to my school classroom to plan my lessons for the next week. After that I returned home and prepared to go to South Post Chapel for the *Living Fire* Christmas Program. It consisted of the choir members singing from a gigantic lighted Christmas tree which was specially constructed. It was beautiful.

9 December 1990

This day, too, was spent in class, 9 a.m.-4 p.m. After class I returned to my school classroom to grade papers. I returned home to do more paperwork and to wrap some gifts for my *Secret Santa*. I am retiring early.

10 December 1990

This is my first working day in seven days, although on Thursday and Friday morning I did stop in to see the class.

It was a very busy day. I noticed that the class had become very noisy and active. This was due in part to my absence and the nearness of the Christmas holiday. After school, I held a calligraphy class which went well. We wrote letterheads on stationery.

I came home and spent the rest of the evening here. I went to bed at 6 p.m. and woke at 12:40 a.m. to finish some paperwork.

11 December 1990

I spent the day in a computer training course. I came away at the end of the day not knowing much more than I did before the session, but I did receive a lot of training material which I will try on my own.

At lunchtime I went to pick up my mail. There was a card from Alice Donstan and a letter from Ganzette Brown, a teacher's assistant at Overview School. She said that my former principal had been promoted to coordinator of instruction for Area II. A box of my decorative plates which were sent to a lady in the States was returned to me opened evidently by the post office. I will have to inquire about this tomorrow.

After school I met with Bridget Tower and Amy Smart of OEA to plan for a minority leadership training session. I remained on after the meeting to do some work in my classroom.

I was glad to get home. Tony called again. I told him I would be busy all week.

12 December 1990

We had a busy day. After school the fifth and sixth grade teachers met with Ms. Bradley, the language development teacher, to help her iron out kinks in our schedules. It was resolved easily. Ms. Bradley just wanted the attention. For the little good her program was doing, I was not willing to make the adjustment she suggested.

I left school, went to Main Post to the Education Center to get a form to send for my NTE results (National Teacher's Exam) which I took in 1963/1964.

On the way home, I stopped at the Dragon Hill Lodge's Oasis for a light supper. I also stopped at Northwest Airlines desk to apply for PERKS, earned free trip for miles traveled. I had a feeling I should have turned it in while in flight. It was cold outside, so I headed for home.

Since I don't have my car, I often ride the post bus. It is an old rickety bus. You are in danger riding it. The seats are uncomfortable and when you get on or get ready to get off, the bus jolts you so that your safety is at risk.

13 December 1990

It has turned quite cold. It warmed up a little in midday, but the temperature dropped again toward evening.

I tried to cram in all the subject matter I could. The principal dropped into my room today for a few minutes. The children were busy. After school I met with Kate, Kathy, Iris and Lorna Skye, travel coordinator, for a briefing on our trip to Bangkok, Singapore and Hong Kong.

I was disappointed that Edna couldn't do my typing. She said she had to go to the States on Sunday. It was probably because of her mother's illness. After making a few calls and not being able to find anyone to type my paper, I called my instructor to see if I could handwrite my paper. He said I could.

14 December 1990

It is Friday, one week before our winter vacation. The day has been a noisy, busy one. It seems that these children are not used to structure. I imagine with teachers coming from everywhere, with different teaching styles and not staying long enough to build a solid foundation, I can understand why. The children do not like to study. They don't put forth much effort unless highly pressured by their parents.

After work I went to Main Post bank to get a bank check for my trip to Bangkok, Singapore, and Hong Kong, December 22nd to December 30th. I delivered the check to Lorna Skye, our travel agent, at the high school. From there I went to Dragon Hill for a light meal.

I went to school to do a little work before it got dark. Incidentally, it snowed last night. The snow stuck only to the railings and the grass.

15 December 1990

I spent 9 a.m. until 4 p.m. in class. After class I came home, had a snack and called Edna to see if she still wanted to go to dinner. I called Hartell House, the exclusive club that I joined, to make reservations, but the dining hall was closed for a private affair. So, we went to the Main Post for dinner in the dining room. Edna was about to leave for the States on Sunday because her mother's condition had changed.

16 December 1990

This is the last day of my three-weekend course. I arose about 6:30 a.m., took a shower, ate breakfast and watched Dr. Benjamin and his congregation out of Indiana. He is a dynamic speaker and his choir sings well. It is a very large congregation and the women wear such lovely hats. Dr. Benjamin's message is always so timely.

I went to class, made my report and took the test. I left about 4 p.m. to return home to unwind. It was then that I wished I had family with me.

I am beginning to think of my goals for the new year. Two of them are to resume weekly fasting and to begin exercise classes. I also plan to pay off my car. I am hoping that Tavia and Gerald will set some goals and work toward accomplishing them.

The assistant principal, Warren Pike, asked me to start another calligraphy class since there were some funds available. I will.

17 December 1990

The day went well. Christmas videos had been scheduled for the entire week. I had planned to have the class view *Currier and Ives Christmas*, but it consisted of only music with scenes and the students didn't like it so I went on with my reading and allowed them to watch *Red Skelton's Christmas* later in the day. I took some small wine flasks to school for the children to make vases. It was done by simply covering the bottle with bits of masking tape and polishing the taped bottle with brown shoe polish. The bottle surface is polished to a glow. I only have about six bottles and all the students want to make one. So I will have to get my friends to save their wine bottles.

After school I held my calligraphy class. The members lettered another type of letterhead and wrote a Christmas message on a piece of paper with a Santa drawing on it. I also allowed each one to select a book or an ink pen as a Christmas gift from me.

We received our pay stub, so I went to the bank to find out if my check was there, only to find the bank closed. It was open from 9:30 - 3:30 on military payday. I am still not sure exactly when their pay days are. I believe they are the 1st and the 17th. I got some won from the money machine, then headed back to Main Post.

The weather was quite brisk. In fact there were snow flurries. I went to Dragon Hill Lodge on the lower level for dinner at the Oasis. I returned home where I stayed for the evening. This is the second evening that I was able to come home, unwind and relax. It is a great feeling.

I thought of Edna who probably was at home in High Point, North Carolina by now with her ailing mother. I empathize with her after having gone through the same thing with Mama six months ago. Death to me causes one to value and appreciate life more. This will be a different Christmas for our family. I hope we will all live through it. Mama will not be with us and I will not be at home. Gerald is planning to go home, but the entire family will not be together. I thought of Marian, my sister, as she battled with cancer and everything else that she had gone through, including the death of Junior, her son. I thought of Beth, my sister. She is so generous and helpful, but her behavior stops her from realizing the good within her. I know she suffers because she feels that she is not appreciated, but that is not so. I wish she would have taken better care of herself physically. I'm grateful to her for what she has done for me. I hope Tavia and Gerald are, too.

I thought of Stanley. He is my brother and I love him dearly. I want to be there for him, too. I thought of Jenny, my sister. She has her children at heart and does everything for them although she feels, too, at times that they don't appreciate her. I hope Jennifer, her daughter will finish college. She is so talented and she can make that talent work for her.

I thought of Peggy, my sister, and Kenneth. Peggy wants the best for her son, Kenneth. She continues to shelter him. I believe her nagging of him has been her downfall. If you continue to fuss at a child constantly, day after day, year after year, the child will tune you out. She has good intentions and means well.

I thought of Joyce, my niece. Although she appears happy on the outside there is some hurt there. After going through two marriages and several failed relationships there must be some grief. I regret that she and Ada, my sister, could not have been closer. They could benefit so much from each other.

I thought of Tavia. I wish that as the new year approaches, she will focus on making life comfortable for her and Tia. Like Peggy, I was hoping she would talk less and focus on herself spiritually, emotionally, and financially. She is as good as gold and I feel she has suffered enough. I want the best for her, but being there every moment for her is not helping her to grow and to help herself. I wish she could find a nice male friend and enjoy life.

I thought of Gerald and how the Lord has blessed him in his travels and his job. I wish for him a challenging and rewarding life.

I wish for Tia a full fruitful life. She is so bright and in time she will do well. I thought of myself and the opportunities that have been afforded me and I praise God for them. I want to live a long time because there is still much I want to do for my family and myself.

I thought of Stanley. I sent him items that he might enjoy having. He told me that every morning when he wakes up he looks at the picture of Mama and Daddy. He thinks of them often.

I told him that I did, too. I feel that we were not as close to them as we could have been or maybe we were, I don't know. Stanley's life lacked much but he is so much better off than most people. He has family, shelter, a job, and he can rest most of the night with little cares. He is most concerned with the news, Mama, Daddy and I guess his job. He also has to contend with Beth's harshness.

18 December 1990

Today the class went ice skating. Some pupils stayed home because they couldn't skate. Two of my students came without permission slips, so I had to try to contact their parents for permission. On top of that, Vance from Guam, didn't bring his inhaler. I was going to allow him to go and not skate, but the administrator advised me not to let him go without it, so I had him to remain with Ted Points, another fifth grade teacher. We then went on our way. We got there about forty minutes early, so we watched the little children taking skating lessons. The ones who couldn't skate tried anyway and had fun. The other teacher and some of the parents skated.

I learned from the assistant principal that Vance Millo's mother was upset that her son was not allowed to go. The nurse called her to say that she informed the school of her son's asthma.

19 December 1990

Vance Millo's mother sent me a letter stating that she was disappointed that her son couldn't go to the ice skating rink. The principal requested a conference with the nurse and me to discuss it.

This is the third day that I have not received any mail. I am worried.

20 December 1990

This was a lively day. First, the nurse and I met with Beatrice Knoy, the principal, regarding the mother and her son who was not allowed to go ice skating because he didn't have his inhaler. The children were very excited. We finished covering the bottles to make them into vases. We had our Christmas party which consisted of Picture Scramble, Christmas music, exchanging gifts and eating pizza, ice cream, punch and cupcakes. I received several nice gifts including a musical card. Nicole gave me a lovely mask hanging.

Christmas will be quite different this year for my family. I will be praying for the welfare of everyone.

21 December 1990

I didn't go to work. The trip organizer had planned for us to leave on December 24th, but as it turned out we were to leave on Saturday morning. Since I have already requested the day off, I will take it.

I sent a few pages of my diary to Tavia, checked the mailbox at school, and went to the post office.

I went to school to check on things and found some more lovely Christmas gifts.

I returned home to relax. At 5:30 p.m. Katie and I went to Hartell House for the *Happy Hour* and dinner. This was my first dinner as a new member and so it was free. The atmosphere was classy. Selena, Jackie, our music teacher, and another friend were there. There were several faculty members there also. I ordered the butterfly shrimp dinner. It consisted of shrimp, french fries, salad, wine and coffee. We passed up dessert. Our dinner reservation was for 6 p.m. We were finished at 7:30 p.m.

22 December 1990

We left for Bangkok at 10:30 a.m. from Kimpo Airport. We ran into Aretha Brough, Mary Smit, Sharon Reid and Louise Tate. Iris Turner and Katie Zinns came later with their boyfriends.

We cleared customs, flew to Taipei for a short stopover, then on to Hong Kong where we changed planes to go to Bangkok. As usual we were fed quite well. When we arrived in Bangkok, it was getting dark, so we couldn't see much. The hotel was lovely. There were people of just about every nationality. We changed clothes and then went to the lounge for our complimentary drink. There was a singer who had a beautiful voice and sang the most popular American songs. We ran into Sandra Carver and her husband. They had arrived the day before. They had their twenty-month-old son with them who was a brat. How they would enjoy this vacation with him, I don't know!

23 December 1990

We left this morning to go on a tour of the city and the temples. It was fascinating -the Buddhas, temples, pagodas, people and food. Our tour also took us to a lapidary company that had some of the finest stones in the world. We also saw the stones being shaped, cut, polished and set. We left there and took a van to the India Hotel where we had a fine vegetarian lunch. From there we went across the street to a bank to get some baht, which is Thai money. I then purchased a Rolex watch.

24 December 1990

We scheduled an early morning tour to the floating market, Damanersaduak and the Rose Garden Tour. The tour started at 6:30 a.m. We did, however, have time for a quick breakfast. Our guide was a very handsome Thai who spoke English well and was very knowledgeable. The trip was a two-hour ride to the river. On the way we passed many interesting places and people. The monks of all ages were on the streets begging food. It was interesting to know that monks are not committed for a lifetime. Some start training at age seven and are called novices. They are not known as monks until age twenty. Even a married man with children can become a monk. He can enter the order and leave at will.

The children were already at school before 7 a.m. They all wore uniforms of blue/black skirts and pants with white shirts and blouses. Yesterday Katie and I took a ride on an open air taxi called a *tuk-tuk*. It was a two-seater plus the driver. It was a rough reckless ride so we had to hold on for dear life. The driver dodged in and out of traffic terribly. Our lives were in the driver's hands. At the riverside we boarded a water taxi and sailed about five miles to the floating market area. We passed houses that were built on stilts. Some people were washing in the river and doing things around the house. Imagine coming out of the house down to your car boat and floating wherever you wanted to go. There were also side rivers. We saw ladies in boats with their goods. We disembarked and bargained with the people on the boats. I purchased a cone-shaped Thai hat, then walked around the shopping area. There were lovely things everywhere. We then boarded the bus to go to Rose Garden, the name of which is misleading, because there were few roses, more orchids than anything. At Rose Garden we had a delicious lunch of vegetable soup, a rice dish, a vegetable dish with beef, another vegetable dish, more rice, chicken, coffee and papaya, and pineapple for dessert.

Following this scrumptious meal we went to the Thai Village show. There we saw traditional dances such as the finger dance, a dance of welcome and greeting where the dancers wear long gold finger nails. There was the bamboo reed dance where the dancers danced between clapping bamboo reeds. There were other dancers accompanied by different types of musical instruments. We witnessed a Thai boxing match. The Thai boxer uses all parts of the body to fight. We saw a sword fight, a cockfight and a traditional wedding ceremony. There was a processional that included a large elephant. From there we went to see the elephant show. It was fun. People volunteered to lie on the ground while the elephants stepped over them. We walked about the shopping area where there were excellent wares. We watched a silversmith, a weaver and a farmer at work. Then we headed for the bus.

Prior to visiting Rose Garden we went to a cobra show. There we saw young men entertaining with various snakes. With one snake, we were shown how venom is extracted from the head of the snake. The snake man was squeezing some venom into a plastic cup. We were told that one drop of the venom could kill an elephant. We were shown the two penises that a snake has. On another snake we were shown its fangs up close. We were also allowed to touch the snake, which I did. A snake was then placed in a cage with a mongoose. The mongoose fought him furiously. The young man then brought out three baby pythons which he let loose, he then caught one in each hand and the third in his mouth. We saw how snakes can be charmed. As we left the show there were young men walking around with snakes around their neck. It was exciting to say the least. I purchased a bottle of water, then boarded the bus. On the bus we were served sugar cane, pineapple and bananas. Some of the bananas were only about three inches long.

    We arrived at the bus station and then took a cab back to the hotel. We rested awhile and then decided to have a light dinner at the hotel. Lord Jim's, a restaurant at the Oriental Hotel, was expensive, $50.00 a dinner plus a surcharge.

25 December 1990

I awoke at the hotel at 6 a.m. and finished packing. This allowed enough time for breakfast. All breakfasts were included in the tour package. We boarded the van to go to the airport for a 11:50 a.m. flight to Singapore. The customs agency had to check my overnight bag because the scanner picked the image of a tiny knife. It turned out to be my fingernail file. As Katie, Kathy, Iris and I rode to the airport, ate breakfast and waited in the lounge we talked of Christmas and our families at home. It was a sad time for us. We were wondering what they were doing. I thought of Tavia at home without me. I was hoping that Gerald was able to come home safely. Everyone everywhere wished us a Merry Christmas. The area was decorated, Christmas dinner served, and Christmas music played. It was a joyous time of the year, but I missed home and the family.

I am writing today aboard our Pacific flight going to Singapore. The pilot has informed us that we are flying at an altitude of 41,000 feet at a speed of 540 miles per hour. The temperature in Singapore is 86 degrees. We crossed the Gulf of Thailand. I have just finished a delicious lunch of fish, rice, vegetables, a beef salad, roll and butter, coffee, white wine and Thai coconut custard pie.

I am hoping that this will be a blessed year for Tavia and Gerald and that they will work toward making life comfortable for themselves. I am hoping Tavia will not get into any more debt than is necessary, that she will keep Tia well and safe, and that she will look out for her well-being. She has the attributes of an outstanding person, but must work toward channeling her talents and abilities in the best way. One must travel through life with alternatives, if one thing doesn't work then one should try another. In this way disappointments will be easier to take.

26 December 1990

The check-in at the airport was fine and the ride to York Hotel was great. The city is so clean and beautiful. It is so busy and English is spoken for the most part. We had a lovely morning tour of Singapore and an afternoon tour of Sentosa Island. We rode a bus to the dock where we boarded a ferry bus to get to the island, then got on the monorail to tour the island and returned by cable car. Some traveling! Of course we shopped and shopped and shopped!! We visited Little India where there is a high concentration of East Indians. We then toured Chinatown. I made purchases in each area. I bought a floor mat in Little India and a pair of shoes in Chinatown. I also visited a mosque in Little India and posed with one of the holy men there.

27 December 1990

We traveled on to Hong Kong. What a difference! I was uneasy in the airport because there were so many army military policemen. Everyone is watched. I was glad when we got through there. We were met by our travel guide as we were at the other airports. I was very impressed with them.

28 December 1990

In Hong Kong we took a morning tour. We stayed on the Kowloon side. The bus took us through the tunnel to the island where we took a tram halfway up Victoria Peak. Victoria Peak is approximately 18,000 feet high. We also took a ride on the Bampan (a small boat) to ride around the fishing village where the boat people live. We also visited a jewelry factory and observed skilled craftsmen making jewelry. Adjacent to it was the jewelry store. It was a rich man's land. We shopped around Hong Kong and found some reasonably priced items and we found some things that only the rich can afford.

29 December 1990

We rode the ferry across Victoria Bay to sleep at China Fleet Navy Center which is military operated. I purchased some ceramics, t-shirts, a fan, an abacus, and a birthday card.

I tasted many kinds of food. We even went to a Thai vegetarian restaurant and an Indian restaurant.

It was fun and challenging spending three types of currency. In Bangkok a U.S. dollar was equal to 25 dollars. In Singapore a U.S. dollar was equal to $2.50. In Hong Kong a U.S. dollar was equal to $7.80. I kept samples of each.

I am writing in my small hotel room while waiting for Katie and Iris to go to dinner. I am having a great time, but I am ready to return to Korea. I want to hear from home to know how everyone is doing.

30 December 1990

Today is Sunday, a day of leisure and one we will spend mostly shopping.

I arose about 5 a.m. Iris and I walked to a nearby park behind a mosque to watch the people of Hong Kong engage in what is called T'ai Chi. It is a slow moving exercise. It is performed by a large group of people to music. There were also some small groups. It looked so beautiful and refreshing that I decided to take pictures. We took pictures. We also saw a small group of people engaging in some type of praise or worship that included speaking and chanting. It reminded me very much of the early praise service that the Baptists engage in. It was refreshing walking along the quiet empty streets of Hong Kong. It was a little scary too in that it was still dark. In fact the hotel guard had to unlock the door for us. It was comforting to know that such a protective measure was taken.

By the time I returned to the hotel, Kathy was awake. We got dressed and had breakfast. Afterwards, we walked to Nathan Road to Saint Andrews Anglican Church. Hong Kong is under British subjection and will be returned to China in 1997.

The officiator spoke beautiful British English. The speaker was Reverend Yates from Falls Church, Virginia. He was very lengthy. The music was beautiful. We sang such songs as *Amazing Grace, Leaning on the Everlasting Arms,* etc. After service there was a coffee and tea hour. I met a black business man, Al Ewell, who had a business in Hong Kong and had been there for three years. He was in international finance and had taught at Howard University and American University.

We went back to the hotel to finish packing since we had to check out by noon. We did so, then walked to McDonald's for a milkshake. In Singapore, there is a K-Mart, a Burger King, Penney's and, of course, McDonald's. While we were waiting in the lounge to be picked up by our tourist coordinator, Katie came rushing in screaming that someone had grabbed her purse with her passport, traveler's checks, camera and other things. Luckily, she had brought another passport and her plane tickets were still in the safe deposit box. I had put my things in a safe deposit box in Bangkok and Hong Kong also. The hotel people were very helpful, they called American Express to cancel her credit card and to apply for travelers' check replacements.

We were finally on our way back to Korea. When I got to the airport, my luggage was overweight, so I went to the ladies room and threw out some of my summer clothes. Then when I got to the scanner, I ended up leaving my woven mat I had purchased in Bangkok. I reported it to *lost and found.*

We boarded the plane for a three-hour flight to Korea. Everything else to this point had gone well. I arrived at my BOQ at about 10:15 p.m. I wanted to call the States to see how everyone was but the phone was dead. This upset me sorely. I checked my phone bill and it indicated that I had until December 30th to pay. Well, I went to bed with that on my mind. But before I went to bed I cleaned out my luggage and displayed the items I had purchased.

31 December 1990

I read and had coffee. I decided to pick up the phone to check it one more time and would you know it, it was working. I called Tavia and she said everything was fine and that Gerald had arrived in Virginia safely. I praised God for that.

I went to school to pick up my mail, then returned to my BOQ when Gerald called. He was doing fine, except for his landlady's objection to his paying her rent with a money order.

I spent the remainder of the day doing little things around my BOQ and reading the paper. I opted not to go to the New Year's Eve worship, but prayed to God at midnight. I attempted to call Marian, my sister, but all the lines were busy.

1 January 1991

The first day of the new year was a quiet one. I awoke about 8:30 a.m. and spent some time in bed reading. I arose, had breakfast and did some paperwork. I then put on my clothes, went to the mailbox, and to the school to pick up some tape. I came home and cleaned out some drawers. Prior to leaving the house, I called Marian, my sister, and she wanted to talk at length. I had to remind her that calling from Korea is quite expensive. I had her to hang up and call me back since it is cheaper to call from the States. She and John were doing fine. Amira was busy preparing for her wedding. She had registered her silver and china at a local store.

I decided to walk to Dragon Hill Lodge at about 5 p.m. It was a nice break away from home. When I returned home I did some schoolwork and started putting my materials together for my upcoming mask presentation if and when Ned sends the masks.

2 January 1991

It is the second day of the New Year. I spent the morning at home doing paperwork. I ate breakfast, then went to school to check my mail. I couldn't get my mailbox open, so the postal worker handed me my mail. I was elated that one of the two pieces of mail was from Troy State University. I earned an A in the course I was taking. The other piece of mail was a Christmas card from Allison Smith of Alston Street Baptist Church. I then went to Main Post to pick up snapshots of my trip and to pick up the note cards I had printed with a picture of the school on them. I was pleased with the work although the envelopes could have been of better quality. I brought them home, had lunch, then went to school to work. I rearranged the desks as I do each month, put up a math display of a fraction chart, fraction parts, money from Canada, Jamaica, U.S.A., Korea, Bangkok, Singapore, and Hong Kong and also a Chinese abacus that I purchased in Hong Kong.

I returned home and began packaging my note cards. I packaged 16 packs of tens, then took a break and called Edna. She talked at length. As soon as I realized I was in for a long conversation I immediately took out a bundle of cards and started folding them as I listened to her, so as not to waste time. I recall I used to do this with Mrs. Donstan, stateside. I would always find something to do, particularly, painting as I listened to her long winded conversation.

3 January 1991

I awoke to a very cold temperature. I arose about 8:50 a.m. read, and had breakfast of cold cereal and tea. I checked my mailbox and received a mailing from Hartell House with two coupons for a discount on an evening meal. I also went to 121 hospital for an electrocardiogram (EKG) and to have my prescriptions filled. I caught the post bus and took a tour of the base, then went to the shoppette to purchase some scotch tape for packaging my note cards.

I entered the family care center at 2 p.m. and had my hair done, my nails and my eyebrows shaped. The workers in the hairdresser were very slow. I left there at 5 p.m. When I got outside it had been snowing! There were about three inches of snow on the ground. I hurried home and took a picture of my first snow in Korea.

Karen called earlier to invite me to her BOQ for a light supper. I had just enough time to freshen up before going there. It was rather slippery outside. When I arrived, Nancy Benton was there. I presented Karen with the first package of note cards. Nancy purchased a pack. I decided to sell them for $3.50.

Karen served a fruit platter with a cream cheese and marshmallow dip. This was followed by a stir fry dish of carrots, chicken chunks, celery, green peppers, and onions served over rice. For dessert we had blueberry cheesecake which was left over from Karen's birthday dinner. We had German coffee, mint tea and soda to drink. I left there about 10:30 p.m. It was cold and icy. I made it home safely and called Karen to let her know that I did.

4 January 1991

It seemed as though I was awakening later and later each day. I awoke at 9:30 a.m. I read, ate breakfast and went to check my mailbox and to go to Main Post. I received two more Christmas cards, one from Everlyn Gross and the other from Maya Roan, a Washington artist who had a show at Ned's gallery in October. Her works sell for thousands of dollars.

I went to Main Post to the Education Center to pick up requests for transcript forms. I saw one of the students from my class. Judging from her conversation, I don't think she earned an A.

It was very, very cold out. Snow was on the ground and it was quite icy. Road conditions had been telecast all night and all day. The streets were very slippery. I was so happy I didn't have to drive.

I had planned to go to *Happy Hour* at Hartell House, but upon leaving my classroom and facing the cold I decided not to do that. The temperature had dropped terribly. So I returned home and wrapped 10 packs of note cards.

I hoped Gerald returned to California safely. There was flooding across the country. If all went well, he should have gotten there by Friday. I hoped his leave didn't jeopardize his work.

I failed to mention in my report of my vacation trip that in flying from Hong Kong to Bangkok and back from Hong Kong to Korea that I flew over a portion of Vietnam. Also in Bangkok, I rode in a Mercedes cab with a uniformed driver. I understand that in Germany the standard cabs are Volvos and Mercedes, which is understandable.

5 January 1991

This was another cold day and I have been inside most of it. I read, packed my notes, studied my lessons for teaching, worked on my income taxes and baked a rice pudding. I left the BOQ to mail a small gift to Jennifer, then up to the Main Post to the printer's to get some envelopes. The printer said he will have them for me on Monday afternoon. I returned home, had dinner and spent the evening working on my income taxes, watching T.V. and planning what I would wear to work next week.

I finished working on my income taxes for 1990 and I found I made a profit on my art business.

I thought of Mama today as I always do. I thought of how I would call her on the day I was to leave on a trip and she would always say "I hope you have a safe trip." Somehow, I believe that her prayers are with me.

6 January 1991

This was a rather quiet day and I spent it alone. I usually have to run the shower water for a length of time before it gets hot when the temperature is low, but this morning, it got hot right away. I dressed to go to service at South Post Chapel. Selena called at about 10:10 to say that she was going to 11 o'clock service at the Main Post chapel. Since I was already dressed I opted to go to South Post. It was communion Sunday and I was glad of that. One of the visitors to the service said he was from Baltimore, Maryland. I spoke to him after service and found out that he lived in Baltimore only two years. He was traveling throughout the East. He was an elderly man, most likely a retiree. He didn't say.

I returned home, had lunch, then went to school. I spent most of the time training myself on the computer since there was a training disk in the package. I stayed there about two and a half hours.

I spent the rest of the evening at home doing more schoolwork, exercising, cooking and watching T.V. I called Kathy to find out if she would be interested in attending an overnight prayer retreat on January 18-19. She was elated. So we both called and made reservations.

I was watching Community Calendar on T.V. when they announced an audition time for the play *Purlie* to be presented in February in conjunction with Black History Month. I then called Selena to see if she would be interested in auditioning. She said she would if she could be in the background. We were going to give it a try. Edna was concerned that the planners were just auditioning. She said when she participated in *Purlie* in Germany, they started rehearsing in September because there is so much music to learn.

7 January 1991

When the alarm went off at 5:30 a.m. I was still sleepy, so I reset the clock for 6 a.m. I awakened still sleepy, but I knew I had to get up and so I did. I read, ate breakfast, dressed and started to leave for work. As I approached the outside door, I looked out of the window to find that the ground was completely covered with snow and it was still coming down. I went back to my BOQ to change my shoes and coat and to get my umbrella. I met up with Nancy Benton and we walked to school together. I went inside the school and then went over to the main building to give Mr. Pike a copy of my grade and to put my note cards on display. I returned to class to find that several children had come. By 8:30 a.m. all but one child had come to school. I had the children to share their vacation experiences. Few of them did. They had so much that they took everything for granted. It seemed nothing excited them anymore. We had reading and then our five week spelling bee. It snowed just about all day. School was dismissed at 1 p.m., one hour early. At that time the snow had stopped and the sun was shining. The children could have stayed another hour. I worked until 2 p.m. I then went to Main Post to put some film in the photo shop and to get a schedule of graduate classes from the Education Center. I returned home, had dinner, then began my twenty-four hour fast. I called Selena to cancel on going to audition for the play *Purlie*. She wasn't very enthusiastic about it, either.

Tony called again this evening. I told him I was expecting company. We chatted for a few moments.

Today's Jenny's birthday. I wonder how she is celebrating it.

8 January 1991

This was another cold, cold day. I got another student, Sherrie Barns from Ohio. This was her first day with DODDS. I had a conference scheduled, but the parent didn't show up. I was happy to leave work today with nothing particular to do and no place to go.

Selena called about 4:30 p.m. to see if I wanted to go to Itaewon. I told her I would have to pass because it was too cold. She said she would stop by about 5:15 to pick up a small gift I brought her from Hong Kong. I broke my fast at 5:30 p.m. and had a big dinner. I then decided to cut some paper towels for my African mask presentation. I was praying that Ned would be able to get the masks to me with no trouble.

Selena stopped by about 6:15 p.m. with her daughter, Tura, who was visiting her from the States. They stayed awhile and left about 7:30 p.m.

9 January 1991

Today was just another ordinary workday. Nothing special happened. I received my mail from Tavia. In it were Christmas cards. I hung them on my door with the others.

I sold six more packs of note cards. I received so many compliments on them.

The teachers were invited to a Teacher's Appreciation Evening at the Embassy Club. It was quite an event. I arrived at 6 p.m. and stayed until 8:30 p.m. It was nice, indeed.

10 January 1991

The day was a quiet one. I had to go to a science workshop at 1:15 p.m. I received my mail from Tavia. I went home and spent the rest of the evening there grading papers, doing some calligraphy and working on my mask presentation. I was praying that the masks would arrive sometime in February.

11 January 1991

This was the end of the first school week in the new year. I sold four more packs of cards. Edna purchased 3 packs last night. I sold $83.00 worth this week. I needed to sell about 13 more packs to cover the cost of printing them.

A fifth grader picked Jeffrey up and threw him down during lunch time. He had to go to the health clinic. Jeffrey is extremely playful. Crystal brought in yesterday's reading paper with all correct responses. I couldn't grade it. Reading is to be done at school. Her parents probably didn't like it, but this was only fair to the other children. I thought, "No wonder she got A's last year." Ben informed me that his teacher gave them the answers to the test the day before the test. No wonder he got A's. What was the purpose in having pupils to read and participate in discussions? No wonder their comprehension was so poor.

I received two Christmas cards from Gerald. I was very relieved to know that he did get back to California all right and he was still working. I immediately went home and addressed his gift package and sent it to him.

I also received a letter from Eugene, the Liberian student who stayed with me for a few weeks a few years ago. It was a blanket letter pointing out his heavy work load and asking for help. I wasn't clear what he needed help in or for.

I went to the school mailbox and picked up a copy of the OEA Journal. In it was an article on the minority conference that I attended in Delaware in December. There was a group picture and my name was highlighted several times.

I went home, ate a light dinner of a salad because I gained so much weight in December. Edna and I planned to go to *Happy Hour* at Hartell House at 6 p.m. When we got there at 6:15, the folks had eaten all the food. It looked as if it was quite a spread. *Happy Hour* starts at 5:30 p.m. Edna said we should arrive at 5 p.m., when the food is placed on the table. There was a lady at the piano, and a few other people standing around, including a woman singing church songs.

Edna and I decided to leave and go to Whispers in Dragon Hill Lodge. It was crowded, but a group of people at one of the tables was leaving, so we were in luck as far as getting a table. I ordered a strawberry daiquiri and some yok min, a meat stuffed dough, which is dipped in a sauce. The D.J. started playing some hillbilly music. Then a few people went up to him and he changed to some dance music. Selena came in. She was depressed at home, so she had come out to rent two videos. I invited her to join us in Whispers. She did and was she glad she did. She talked and danced and appeared to be enjoying herself. She remained there after we left. I danced with a fellow, Rickey, from Murfreesboro, N.C. near Wilson, N.C. He ordered me a drink. I chose a Coke.

We left Dragon Hill about 11:30 p.m. Ricky and another fellow walked us to the car. Edna went home with me to purchase three packs of cards.

12 January 1991

I ate an early lunch and graded some social studies papers. I called Edna to find out if she was still going to the free calligraphy class which started at Moyer Recreation Center. She was.

It was a large class with an enrollment of 40. The instructor was very good. He said he had been teaching calligraphy classes for ten years. I could only stay for one hour because I had to attend the T.E.A.K. meeting, so I left at break time. I was sitting beside a sniffling guy who needed to blow his nose. I was tempted to offer him a tissue. I recognized him as a fellow I met when we first arrived in Korea who offered to give Selena, Kathy and me a ride. He said he wanted to be a teacher sponsor, but couldn't. So he offered to help in any way he could.

On the way out, I stopped in the arts and crafts shop to buy some raffia. I had high hopes that I would be able to do my mask presentation here.

I walked over to South Post to the ROTC building where the meeting was being held. As I entered the room, I was attracted to the large spread of food and vowed that I wouldn't eat anything sweet. I opted for a diet soda and a couple of crackers.

I had to report my plans for our Minority Leadership Training Workshop, although I came prepared to talk about my trip to the States for the seminar.

The meeting was dismissed at 3 p.m. It was still very cold, so I vowed to go home and stay in for the rest of the evening.

There was talk about restrictions which would go into effect at midnight January 15th because of the war in the Persian Gulf. It was very frightening. When I got home there was a telecast on about the Korean War. Why they chose this time to air it, I don't know.

13 January 1991

As I was getting dressed, the electricity went off. It was off for about 15 minutes. I went to South Post chapel. I returned home, had a snack and finished reading the day's paper.

I went to Main Post for the ceramic workshop. The ceramic workshop was great. We glazed a beer stein using an antiquing technique. The stein was trimmed in gold. The workshop cost $8.00 and lasted for two hours. I left the stein there to be fired.

I returned home and had dinner. As I entered the door, the phone was ringing. I didn't think it was Flowers because I had just seen him. It was Selena. I could tell she wanted company because she wanted to know if I needed anything at the PX or the commissary. I told her I didn't, but after she hung up, I sensed something was wrong, so I called her back.

We rode to Main Post where I picked up my photos, shopped at the PX and browsed at the bookstore. The bookstore was very well stocked.

We left there and stopped at *Whispers*. Selena talked of how her friends had betrayed her, including the chaplain's wife.

After leaving there, I went home and watched *Civil War*. It was still very cold out.

14 January 1991

This was another very cold day. Things went well. Fred, one of my students, was still acting like a fool. He should have never been promoted to fifth grade reading on a third grade level. The mail clerk, Mr. Danson, brought him in after 8 a.m., reporting that his parents' car broke down in Osan last night. I assumed they were up there partying as usual. Fred had spent the night at the mail clerk, Mr. Danson's house.

I held my calligraphy class today. It went well. Everyone worked hard. An emergency staff meeting was held to let us know that the base was on *THREAT COM* and several gates were closed. We were urged to collect and store water for often the water supply is attacked and there had been threats of terrorism.

I finished reading the entire Bible, from Genesis to Revelation on January 10th. I have read it several times. I don't know which reading this is, but I have it recorded in my Bible at home in the States. I think it is the fourth.

15 January 1991

This was the birthday of Daddy and Martin Luther King, Jr. I woke up to a snow-covered terrain. I arrived at school about 6:40 a.m. The children drifted in late because buses were late. It stopped snowing and by mid-day the ground was clearing. The principal had us to bring the children to the cafeteria five minutes early so she could explain the terrorist threat situation. Some base gates were closed and cars were being searched.

After school, I got a ride to Main Post with Tammy Reid. She warned me that the van was a mess. That was putting it mildly. It was a disaster. On Main Post, I went to Moyer Recreation Center to put the gold trimming on my beer stein. I waited for the bus and rode back to South Post to my classroom. The Korean custodians were there vacuuming the floor.

I returned home and checked some papers. I am in my 24th hour of fasting.

16 January 1991

I awoke and turned on the television. There was talk of war, war, and more war. It seemed as though there were wars everywhere. The children drifted in late again today because buses were being delayed. The day went well, though. I received my request for my NTE scores back with a letter stating that scores would not be given after twenty years. I took the tests 27 years ago.

I have no plans for the afternoon and evening and am I glad. I ran off flyers and hand-outs for the Minority Leadership Training Seminar and I will spend the evening sorting those.

17 January 1991

The day was unusual in that we heard that the war in the Persian Gulf had begun. We watched President Bush address the nation on the war situation. It was a direct, thorough, fine speech. An MP (Military Policeman) informed me that there was a bomb threat at the high school.

At lunch time, four of my boys attacked Jeffrey. They were doing something called *dogpiling* where a group of boys jump on and beat another child. The boys said they thought Jeffrey was enjoying it because he was laughing. Jeffrey is a Korean who appears to be smiling all the time, the typical show of his two front teeth.

When I went to the mailbox, I found the mail that Tavia sent me. I appreciate how prompt and expediently she sends my mail. Most of it was junk mail. But also there was a refund check for $223.00. I had paid off my car. I jumped for joy.

At the end of the day, we were informed that schools would be closed for the pupils the next day, but we had to attend.

I spoke to Mr. Shields today about my NTE scores. I hope I won't have to take the tests again.

I also sent the flyers announcing the Minority Leadership Training Seminar out to the FRS (Faculty Representative Spokesman) at each of the schools in Korea.

After school, I got a ride with Selena to Main Post to pick up my beer stein and to go to the bank. My stein was beautiful, but I was a little disappointed that there were a few light smear marks. I plan to make another one January 27th. I think I will make the next one red.

18 January 1991

The children did not have to go to school today and was I glad. I went to work with all intentions of getting a lot done when I was informed that we were having a grade level meeting at 9 a.m. It lasted until 10:30 a.m. There were several interruptions including the news that Iraq had attacked Tel Aviv.

I returned to my room, wrote my lesson plans and planned for a math lesson which would be observed by Ms. Ridgely, the assistant principal, on Tuesday. I chose not to go to lunch with my colleagues because I felt I had wasted enough time. So I went home, had a salad, sandwich and coffee.

Kathy and I are attending a religious retreat that is scheduled for today and tomorrow. We met at South Post chapel to board the bus to go to the 8th Army Religious Retreat Center beyond Itaewon. There were about 40 women. When we arrived we had dinner right away which was very filling. This was the beginning of an *eating* weekend. We went to the conference room where there was more food and drink. We sang songs that I did not know and never heard of. We had a speaker and then broke up into small groups to read a scripture, answer questions and discuss them. We retired to our rooms after eating some more.

19 January 1991

I arose about 6 a.m., took my shower and went back to bed. Since there were all women, we were allowed to use the men's restroom and showers. The hospitality committee had placed cut flowers in the urinals. We were awakened at 7 a.m. by the singing of *We Will Rejoice in the Lord.* This was our wake-up call. There were three ladies walking up and down the hall singing, playing the guitar and banging a tambourine. We had early prayer service, then went to breakfast at eight in the mess hall/dining room. We went to the conference hall for our second session which included singing unfamiliar songs, except one or two, listening to the speaker, Micky Callin, who was from Burke, Virginia, and more small group talk. There was more food. One young lady in my small group was from Baltimore, Maryland. She lived in Dundalk.

    We had lunch at noon and then we went back to the third session. We sang and were dismissed to spend a quiet time by ourselves reading scripture and meditating. I sat on a bench just outside the chapel. We returned for another small group session.

    It was then time for dinner. Before going to dinner we had to move our overnight bags to one central location. Dinner consisted of chicken, lasagna, potatoes, spinach, cauliflower, salad, drinks, and ice cream and cake.

    We went back to the chapel for our fourth and final session. There was more singing, the speaker and small group sessions. I met a Chinese lady who asked me about giving her daughter beginning piano lessons.

    We were asked to evaluate the retreat. The spiritual part was very good. Having attended several retreats, planned and coordinated two myself, I offered several suggestions.

    We boarded the bus at 9:30 p.m. I was very tired. Carolyn Brow, a teacher at school, gave Karen and me a ride home.

    I watched T.V. for the first time in 31 hours. The war was in full force.

20 January 1991

    I decided not to go to church today since I had spent 28 hours at the retreat. I spent much of the morning reading. I went to Main Post to sign up to go to Bear Town Ski Resort. I, however, would not be skiing. From there I caught the Post bus, took a tour of Camp Coiner and went on to the commissary. My intention was to do my shopping before the folks got out of church, but as I was going to the commissary, there they were in their suits and high heels, shopping for groceries. When church is over they all converge on the PX, the Townhouse, the commissary, the main club, everywhere. They come in droves.

I went home and relaxed, then decided I would go to the Martin Luther King Vigil Candle Light March and Memorial Service. It was beautiful. I was so proud of myself for passing up the reception. When I weighed myself yesterday, I had lost a pound.

After the ceremony, Edna took me on a tour of the base. We then stopped in Dragon Hill Lodge to see the new bookstore. We also visited The Gallery where beautiful Korean items are sold.

The weather was great but the temperature was dropping.

21 January 1991

Today was a very busy day. I was awakened by a phone call from Tavia. As usual I was glad to hear from her and to know that things were going as well as they were.

I did some reading and got ready to go to Main Post to board a bus going to Bears Town Ski Resort. I hadn't planned to ski. I spent the day watching the skiers, walking around and eating. I took some good photo shots. I had met the tour guide before. I have taken so many trips that I know them all. There was a ski instructor aboard to assist beginners. We returned to the base at 5 p.m.

When we got back to the base, Karen dropped me off while she checked to see if *Ghost* was still playing at the theater and at what time. I went to my apartment and began preparing a light dinner when Karen knocked on the door. While we ate, another knock came at the door. It was the Korean sewing lady. I had her to measure me for a Thai silk top and a Thai satin dress suit. She charged me 35,000 won which is about $50.00. She would have to buy the zippers, thread and facing. I didn't need to provide a pattern.

After she left, we went to the theater a half hour early. Luckily we did because there was such a long line that we barely found seats. Selena was there with a married fellow, Troy, whom everyone feels she shouldn't associate with. The movie theater began noisily with the audience making comments and wolf calls. The audience did, however, calm down. Carolyn Brow went to get some popcorn and returned without it because the movie had begun and she didn't want to miss any part. I enjoyed this movie starring Whoopie Goldberg. It is interesting that before the movie is shown the audience stands at attention while the national anthem is played on the screen with patriotic scenes.

22 January 1991

The children had a four-day break. I gave them a reading test, so now I can give reading grades. The day was a chilly, rainy one. I went to my mailbox and found a card from Gerald containing two lovely snapshots of himself working in the laboratory. I also received a letter of verification from Ned regarding the cost of the Chi Wara mask which was broken in shipment. The claim agent insisted on my gluing the pieces back together. The mask had been broken into about five or six pieces. I was told that I would receive a check.

I came home with all intentions of spending the evening there.

Incidentally, we had a faculty meeting after school. A man who was an expert on terrorism spoke to us. We were still in stage *Bravo* which had some restrictions. When we move to *Charlie* and *Delta*, it is serious. Beatrice Knoy, our principal, announced that she would be retiring next year and she would move to Florida. Also she told me that since the testing service does not report scores after 20 years, I would have to take the NTE again.

Rosa Ridgely, our assistant principal, was supposed to do a formal observation of me. She was out sick. I was quite disappointed after I had prepared the lesson so well for her.

23 January 1991

When I went out to work, the street was quite icy. Luckily, just beyond my BOQ, there was a fence and a rail. I held on for dear life.

My room got cold around 1:30. So, immediately after school I went to the library to work on my report cards until it became cold there. Then I left to post flyers advertising the Minority Leadership Training Workshop.

Selena called to find out what I was going to bring to the soul food luncheon on Friday. I had mixed feelings about the luncheon being called that. Since the luncheon was to commemorate Dr. King, why not call it a *Dr. Martin Luther King, Jr. Luncheon*? I hadn't planned to participate, but perhaps I will provide some drinks.

24 January 1991

I woke up to a very snowy morning and it snowed all day. The children were dismissed at 1:30 p.m. I had the class to make salt designs and perspective drawings. At lunchtime I checked my mailbox and found a blue jogging suit from Marian which fit me perfectly. I left work and went to Main Post to sign up for the tour of a crystal factory on Saturday.

I caught the bus to go home, but when we got to South Post the street was blocked, so I got off the bus, did a little shopping in the shoppette in Dragon Hill Lodge and started to walk home. I was stopped by an MP who told me the block was off limits. So I went around Dragon Hill climbing a slippery slope. Not knowing where I was, I walked on, cold as could be until I reached home. I later found out that there was a bomb scare at the high school.

I finally got home and ate a light dinner. By then it was time to go to the high school play that Paula Riff's drama class produced. It was nice. There wasn't a full house but all the seats were sold. They kept turning the lights out and I was trying not to go to sleep.

I came home and was all settled in with my pajamas on when Paula knocked on the door. She came to get my reaction to the play. I told her it was great and I enjoyed it tremendously. She said she had to send to the States for the make-up. The make-up was silver and gold. Some of the characters looked as if they were from Star Trek. It was indeed a very professional job.

25 January 1991

Today the children did not have to go to school. It was the end of the quarter and a workday for the teachers, so I went to school and put up a bulletin board on Martin Luther King, Jr. I then proceeded to work on my report cards. Then Selena drove me home to pick up the tuna macaroni dish I had prepared for the luncheon at 11:30 a.m. Only about 15 members of the staff attended. There was lots of food and quite a variety. We had a short program which consisted of the singing of *Lift Every Voice and Sing* and *We Shall Overcome*. Rosa Ridgely read some excerpts from King and Dubois. Afterwards, I worked on my report cards some more.

My cleaning lady said I should call the maintenance people for more heat in my apartment. I did and they came.

It had gotten very cold outside. Snow and ice were still on the ground.

26 January 1991

We awoke to learn that the base was under curfew from 6 p.m. until 6 a.m., which meant we could neither leave nor enter the base during these hours.

I had breakfast, worked on my report cards and then prepared to go to Main Post to board the bus to go on a tour of Parka Crystal. It was interesting. We were shown a video of how crystal is made. We then went into the factory to watch the workers take melted glass and blow it into hold glass just as it showed in the video. We watched as they cut and polished the crystal. We also saw them in the packing process. We then went to the crystal showroom. From there we went to the factory store where I purchased a lovely crystal ice bucket.

I returned to the base to attend a calligraphy class. Selena and Edna were already there.

We then returned to South Post to Dragon Hill Lodge where the MP's were and had blocked the entrance from vehicular traffic. They had police dogs with them. We didn't know what had happened. We browsed around *Whispers* and *Bentley's* before we decided to go downstairs to Oasis for a light lunch of enchiladas and hot tea.

27 January 1991

Today was a very quiet one. I awakened about 5:30 a.m. with my stomach aching. I had cramps for the first time in over a year. I had to call the doctor to see if this was unusual.

I read a story for work, finished writing comments on the remaining five report cards and designed a cover for my minority training booklet. I had breakfast, read the paper, took a shower and went to service at South Post chapel.

I came home, had a light snack and rested. I then went to Main Post Arts and Craft Center to make another beer stein. I glazed this one red. Selena, Edna and the mother of one of my students signed up for the session, but they didn't show up. Virginia Mays, one of my students, was there for the children's art class. Jean, the record keeper for the school, was there making a cut glass design.

I returned home, had a light meal, played my keyboard and watched T.V. I had played the keyboard before I went to Main Post and I had also written Gerald a letter. I thought of Mama and Daddy as I always do. I think of them everyday. I got lonely for home today. I have four and a half more months to go. I thought of Tia. I look forward to seeing her.

28 January 1991

I awoke with severe cramps. It was just like the awful menstrual periods that I suffered for 39 years of my life. I made it through the day with my discomfort. I asked Edna, who is a nurse, if this is unusual. She said that she didn't think so. She felt that it was probably the change of environment, my loneliness for my family and my busy schedule which had caused the onset. She urged me, as I had intended to, to make note of the days of my period and should it occur again next month consult my doctor. I took Pamprin and drank tea.

I finally finished my report cards and turned them in to Rosa. I held my calligraphy class. The pupils wrote their names on patterns to be made into mugs. Marcia Cain, the newspaper sponsor, came to photograph us at work.

I caught a ride with Tammy and Ray Reid to Main Post. I withdrew some won from the bank telemachine to pay my sewing lady when she comes. I also went to the Education Center to register for the NTE. Mr. Pike verified that I really had to take it. It costs $70.00. I returned home and I stayed all evening.

29 January 1991

I awakened with some cramps, so I took Pamprin and made it through the day. Rose Ridgely gave me my report cards and they passed with flying colors. Fred fell asleep twice. I had recommended him for testing and his mother was scared. I blamed her, Fred and Fred's former teacher. Her, for not making Fred more responsible. Fred, for not being responsible and his former teacher for *giving* him high grades rather than having him earn them. He was given *A's* and *B's*. He had scored below the 20 percentile on the California Tests of Basic Skills.

My sewing lady came with my beatiful silk top. As for the two-piece dress, the neck was too tight so she removed the collar and made a bow out of it, then split the side of the top. She also took in the skirt.

30 January 1991

I felt a little better this morning. The day went well. I received a verification of my salary increase which would show up on my next paycheck.

The children received their report cards. I had 15 out of 27 to make the honor roll. I listed their names on the blackboard with their grade point average. I also gave each one a note card with my drawing of the school on it. It was also a promotion gimmick. I hoped the parents would want to buy some packs of my note cards.

After work I went to Main Post to turn in my voucher application to receive funds for temporary lodging before leaving the States. I was hoping to get a check for my mask that was damaged plus the above check the next week. I then went to Moyer Recreation Arts and Crafts Center to paint the gold trimming on my beer stein.

My sewing lady delivered my two-piece dress. It looked gorgeous.

The nurses sponsored a weight loss competition. It cost $8.00 to join. I joined. I needed and wanted to lose some weight before returning to the States.

31 January 1991

This was the last day of the month and I had not missed a work day at all this month. I am debating whether or not to go in tomorrow which is Friday.

I received a thank you card from Jennifer. I sent her a card for her birthday with money and a silver bracelet that I purchased in Bangkok.

I met with Fred's mother after school today. She was so supportive and helpful, but now we need Fred to do his part.

I left work and went to Main Post to the bank to get some won. It feels so good to get paid every two weeks. In Virginia we were paid monthly. I mailed a letter to Gerald and one to Marian. I enclosed money for her to send me another jogging suit.

I returned to South Post to the shoppette to pick up a few groceries. I then came home. I received a call from Kathy inviting me to join her and a party at Sable's for dinner.

1 February 1991

This was the first of February, four and a half months before I will go home, God willing. The day went quickly. I had my children to begin making their Valentine's Day cards. After work I rushed to the beauty salon. I arrived there at 2:35 and left at 6 p.m. I decided to try another beauty salon next time.

Before school started, I went to Edna's room. She had two chests that she wanted to sell. I picked one which was in two parts. I thought I might give it to Tia because I was not sure how I would use it. She wanted $95.00. I persuaded her to take $85.00.

After leaving the beauty salon, I prepared to go to Sable's, an exclusive restaurant in Dragon Hill Lodge. I went with Carolyn Brow, Kathy Jannis and Mary Spat. Just after Kathy took my picture, the camera jammed. I think I got my money's worth out of it. We left Sable's where I ordered shrimp with white wine. The meal was delicious, but not filling. We went next door to Sable's to *Whispers*. It was rocking. I met a fellow just outside the door in the lobby. He wanted to talk, but he wasn't my type. When we got inside I told Carol that we would take the table for two, that way he couldn't join us.

The usual gang was there. Earl, Floyd, Tony and company, Ronda and her husband. Carolyn met a guy who was thirty-nine. He pulled up a chair. She danced several times with him, then decided to go to Itaewon with him to another night club. Carolyn is about my age or older. She has grandchildren. She asked me to go, but I turned her down. Besides, we had a 6 p.m. to 6 a.m. curfew and she lives off base.

I read my horoscope that night and it said to forget about the past, particularly the bad times. Look to now and the future. This is true. I try everyday to be a better person, to analyze myself, and take an assessment of my thoughts about situations.

2 February 1991

I worked on my T.E.A.K. Minority Leadership Training Conference plans. I read the material and wrote a letter of invitation to minority members.

It was the second day of February and I haven't started my walking routine which I made as a new year's resolution, so I vowed to start today. I donned my blue jogging suit and walked around the school campus to Baskin Robbins to inquire of having my class go there on February 14th for a Valentine's Day ice cream party. It would be a little crowded but they would enjoy it.

I returned home and called Selena to see if she was going to calligraphy class. She was. She picked me up at 12:45 p.m. We had two hours of class. Edna arrived just as we did. After class, Selena and I went to the PX, Seoul Friendship Arcade, and the hair salon.

Upon arriving home, Carolyn Brow called to ask if I would like to join her and Kathy at Burger King, at the theater to see Mermaid, and at the Embassy Club. I turned them down for the first two with a possibility of joining them at the Embassy Club.

I laid down to rest, when Edna called me to inform me that the first segment of *Roots* was being aired. I watched as much as I could stand. There were some parts that were so depressing.

3 February 1991

This was the second day of my walk routine. I returned, showered and got ready for church service at South Post chapel. It was communion Sunday. The minister talked about learning being a dangerous thing if one uses it to idolize himself rather than help himself and his fellow man.

After service I walked to Main Post to the tour and travel center. I was on stand-by for a tour of Seoul and the Seoul Tower. At 12 noon, the final passenger arrived, so a gentleman and I waiting could not take the tour. I ran into Tony who had just returned from Osan. He had gone there to pick up a suit he had made. He wanted to know if he could walk with me to the Black History Variety Show. I had no intention of attending. It angered me that the black community was celebrating Black History Month with a variety show, a fashion show and a dance. Couldn't we be recognized for something other than entertainment?

I returned home and had a snack and I then called Jenny, my sister. I was not thinking. It was 3:10 p.m. on Sunday here and 1:10 a.m. Sunday morning there. Sean, her son answered. He had come home for the weekend. He informed me that the second edition of his school newspaper was out. He was assistant editor and would be sophomore class president. I was so proud of him. He was indeed going places.

I spent the rest of the day at home. Edna called me at 6 p.m. to inform me that she would not be delivering the chest that I purchased until tomorrow.

I watched most of the second segment of *Roots*.

4 February 1991

I woke up to a layer of snow, but that wasn't the problem. The snow was very dry and powdery, which made walking easy. The problem was my noisy class. It was as though everyone of them was *high*. I had no control over them whatsoever. I'd tell them to get quiet and it was as if they were deaf. Besides that, over half of them had colds and they were coughing in unison. One child had been wearing a t-shirt and going outside with his jacket unbuttoned. He asked if he could go to the restroom which was located outside in another building. When I looked up he was going out in the cold snow with no coat on. I said to myself, "If I make it to the end of the day *sane* I will not come in to work tomorrow."

To add suffering to misery, Edna called to tell me she was bringing the chests over that I promised to purchase from her. I thought that I told her I wanted one set of chests. She brought both sets. She was quite disappointed. I found out from taking the STT course with her that it was very difficult for her to process information. She had to look at my assignments in order to know how to do hers. She could not process information from the instructor.

I had settled down for the night when Paula knocked on the door wanting some salad dressing. She was always borrowing.

Tony just called. He wanted to know if I was busy. I told him I was always busy. He said he'd call back.

5 February 1991

I woke up very sore, weak and coughing. Luckily, I had decided to take the day off. I spent some time in bed and most of the time lying on the sofa. Edna called to apologize for the misunderstanding. At about 11 a.m. I went to work to check my mailbox. At 2:30 p.m. I went back over to the school to check on what the substitute teacher had done, picked up some papers to check and prepared the room for the next day. I returned home and spent the evening resting.

6 February 1991

I awoke feeling very weak again this morning, but I managed to read the newspaper, read my teacher training material and write two experiments.

Selena gave me a ride to the A.C.S. building to check on the status of the mask that was broken. The military guy there was quite nasty. He said when he called there was no such place as Lafayette Gallery. Come to find out Ned had typed the wrong telephone number on the letterhead. He said he would call again.

Depressed, I went to work, picked up more papers to check, planned a science lesson and prepared the room for the next day.

The 6 p.m. to 6 a.m. curfew for Korea had been lifted. I thought we should be careful anyway.

7 February 1991

I returned to work after two days of absence. The substitute had done very well. The children said he was an old man named Stu Ziff. It was a very rainy day, a fine time to be out after a cold.

There were two messages in my box to call the claims office. This Sgt. Slavin called Lafayette Gallery, for what, I don't know. I guessed he didn't believe the letter I brought to him. Ned verified the purchase. He said that there had been damage to the mask prior to it being sent here. One of the antler's had been broken, but the mask arrived in Korea in six pieces. I took the mask with intentions of taking it up with the legal office.

8 February 1991

Friday, thank goodness! Friday was usually a light day. The class watched a very enlightening show titled *Reading Rainbow* narrated by Lamar Burton. Afterwards we had a weekly spelling test. We went to the library to do research on an outstanding Black American for Black History Month. Each child had to research a person. The morning went well. I received a letter from claims telling me about the little money they will give me for the damage to my mask. I asked Nat Nalls, the math teacher, if he knew of any Korean who might be able to repair it. He said he thinks so.

Amy Smart, the T.E.A.K. President, said that we may have to cancel our minority training workshop because not many will attend. I had news for her, I was not canceling anything because I had put too much work into it. And just as she wanted recognition, so did I. Besides this would look good on my resume.

9 February 1991

Saturday morning and I can sleep late. I did some schoolwork, then took a 40-minute walk around the base. I had time to go to Main Post bank to get some won and to purchase a dress to wear to the dance. I also prepared a tuna dish and crackers for the T.E.A.K. meeting. I arrived at the T.E.A.K. meeting at 12:30 p.m. It was held at our school. The meeting went well. I gave my report. The meeting adjourned at about 3:30 p.m.

I returned home, sorted out some materials for my Minority Leadership Training Workshop. By that time, I had to get ready for the United College Fund Drive benefit dance.

I arrived there at about 7:45 p.m. The folks had already arrived for the benefit. By 8:30 p.m. there were wall-to-wall black folks. There were displays of the various sororities and fraternities. The food was great. It was quite a spread. The only negative thing was that there were no plates. We had to put our food on napkins. About 10 p.m. each Greek organization did what is called a *step*. It was the organization's dance step and call. Door prizes were given. Edna won a nice ice bucket. Tony showed up and I avoided him.

10 February 1991

The weather was lovely. I awoke and worked on my T.E.A.K. Minority Leadership Training Seminar project. I then went to South Post chapel. They sang some of my favorite songs. The title was *Left Behind* from Mark 9:2-9. A Korean was baptized by the sprinkling of water.

After service, I came home, changed clothes and took a morning walk around the base. I had a light snack then went to Main Post for a ceramic class. At the ceramic class I made two heart-shaped picture frames. They will be fired and I can pick them up Tuesday.

After the class I went down the hall to the 8th Army Band Concert. Edna and Kathy were there. The band played selections of America songs. I recognized just about all of them. The end was best when they played a medley of patriotic marches.

Edna drove me to Dragon Hill Lodge where I looked for a wedding card and wedding wrapping paper. They had neither, so we went to the shoppette. Edna's mouth was running non-stop all the time.

She dropped me off at home. I came into the house and prepared a light dinner, worked on my training project and fell asleep. When I woke up *Roots* was on. I watched for five minutes then changed the channel. The movie saddened me.

11 February 1991

The children's behavior was a little better today than last Monday. Many have very little task skills and know how to do very little. It was not all their fault. It was the teachers who were not teaching and who were not upholding high standards for them. Fred was still acting up. He brought in an electric pencil sharpener.

I held my tenth calligraphy class and I had eleven present.

After work, I walked for about forty minutes. I received a call from Tavia communicating information from Gerald.

I learned while living here not to rely wholeheartedly on any one person. If I ask someone to do something or for something and there was some hesitation or if they didn't follow through, I immediately look for another source or avenue. Being too dependent on someone else can ruin your life. Get where you're going by yourself. Don't depend on anyone to get you there, not even your family. Above all, be observant of your friends.

The 6 p.m. to 6 a.m. curfew is back on.

12 February 1991

Today is Abe Lincoln's birthday. After work, I went to Main Post to pick up my two heart-shaped ceramic frames. I returned home, ate dinner, then went for my evening walk. I returned home to do some schoolwork and to read the newspaper. I was shocked to read that Reverend James Cleveland had died of a respiratory disorder.

13 February 1991

I had an early morning meeting to discuss putting Fred Proctor, a distracting child in my class, in a special education program. His parents were punishing and beating him to make him do his work, but it did no good.

I met with Amy Smart, president of T.E.A.K., to plan for our Minority Leadership Training Session. She was surprised that I had done so much. I intended to make her aware of my ability to plan, organize and present.

I went to sign up for two weekend tours, but everything was booked. I will try the USO tours on Friday. I also went to price certificates for the training session and found them to be costly.

I came home then walked for about forty minutes.

14 February 1991

Today is Valentine's Day and the beginning of the Korean Luna New Year. It is their New Year's Eve. Tomorrow they will celebrate New Year's Day and everyone will be a year older. This is the year of the sheep.

The day went well. Fred fell asleep again. In the afternoon the class went to Baskin Robbins for ice cream. They sat at the Burger Bar, ate ice cream and sang. This lasted a half hour. Prior to going there, they exchanged cards at school. I received candy, a carnation, a gift box with a metal heart and a personalized I.D. key chain, a sweet delicacy and lots of cards.

I had a parent conference, then came home to change clothes to go to a restaurant for a Lunar New Year dinner. We ate and ate and ate. There were games and singing. We got back from dinner at about 9 p.m.

15 February 1991

Friday at last! It has been raining all day. Fred fell asleep at his desk, woke up and began disturbing the class. I told him to stand behind my desk. When I looked back at my desk a few minutes later, I didn't see him. He was asleep on the floor. Earlier in the day, he had taken off his shoes and socks. Then he wanted to call home for dry socks. He said his mother would bring them at lunch time. His father showed up at about 1:15 with the socks, forty-five minutes before the close of school and just after Fred had awakened.

After work we had cake and roses for Rosa Ridgely's birthday. She was now forty-nine.

I checked my weight and I had lost some pounds.

I went to Magic Mirror to get a relaxer, but the shop was closed. It was the Korean Lunar New Year. The beauty salons are run and operated by Koreans. I went to Family Care at Dragon Hill Lodge. It, too, was closed.

16 February 1991

I awoke rather early for a Saturday morning. I took my morning walk, returned home and had breakfast of wafers and coffee. I then went to the beauty salon, Magic Mirror, because I had become dissatisfied with Family Care at Dragon Hill. The operator took me right away. I got an Optimum mild relaxer, my nails done and my eyebrows shaped. It was a nice quiet atmosphere. My nails cost $4.00 more than Family Care, though.

I left there, returned home, had a quick snack and rode with Edna to Moyer Recreation Center for our calligraphy class. We finished the alphabet and began writing the same alphabet in a smaller size. We wrote things such as our name, the place we were from, etc. The instructor complimented me several times on my writing.

On my way home, I stopped at Dragon Hill Lodge. Rosa Ridgely was there doing some serious gambling. It was her forty-ninth birthday. She was playing two quarter machines and had covered the display on each. I assumed she didn't want to see if she was winning or losing until a certain point.

I came home, had a light supper, wrapped Amira's gift and glued part of my mask. Eureka!!! It stuck.

I went to bed about 7 p.m., woke up and watched *Saturday Night Live*. There was a segment called Darkside hosted by Nat-X. It was a satire on black folks. One of the persons it poked fun at was Colin Powell. It was great.

17 February 1991

I awakened about 7 a.m. and went for a walk at 8 o'clock. I walked for forty minutes. I returned home glued another part of my mask, then went to South Post chapel. The regular chaplain, Chaplain Van Schen, didn't speak. Chaplain Rollins wasn't as thorough. His text was from 1 Peter 3:19-22.

As I was walking home, I came upon Kathy Jannis who was talking to Lil Ellsworth, the superintendent's wife. She invited us to lunch at the Golf Club, where she is a member. It was a lovely time. I ordered Bulgoki, a beef dish with rice. It was delicious. Lil ordered Koak Soo, which was a bowl of noodles with egg, vegetables and meat. Mrs. Ellsworth paid the bill. She wanted some company since her husband was away, as he often is, on school business.

I went to school to do some work, then walked to the beauty salon to make a purchase. By that time I had to go to Main Post to the Army Band Concert. The finale was good. It was called King's Lincoln Memorial. A fellow read King's *Free at Last Speech* against a backdrop of concert music.

18 February 1991

I woke up at about 5 a.m. although we were off for President's Day. I walked for about forty-five minutes. I ate before I left. When I returned I took a nap. It was a very slow day. The tours were booked up because of the holiday. I played some tunes on my keyboard, ate lunch, then went to Dragon Hill Lodge. When I came home it had become very cold. I remained at home and hoped it would snow tonight so we wouldn't have to go to school tomorrow.

I was trying to think of a gift to send Joyce, my niece. I thought I would send her a little delicate fan that I purchased in Singapore. I would go next week to Itaewon to purchase a handbag for her also.

We had some excitement tonight. About 7:15 I heard sirens very near, so I decided to look out the window. Lo and behold the superintendent's office was ablaze. It was located across the street and a few yards down from where I live. The flames were coming from the roof and the smoke smell was awful. Someone said there was a gas leakage. The MP's came and evacuated us. Selena, Joan, Nancy, Paula, Phil, Sam and everybody else went to the hotel. Sam said he hoped his transfer papers didn't get burned. Selena and I decided to go to the PX where I purchased a jacket to wear when I go out walking. It was bright red and washable. We stayed at the PX until it closed at 9 p.m. I returned home and called Edna to give her an update on what had happened.

On the way home, we saw a fellow Selena met at Rosa's house on Wednesday night. He had come over to her place unannounced and uninvited and was waiting for her. She said Rosa invited her to her place Wednesday night and there were seven men there. If this guy was the pick of the crop, Heaven help the others.

I failed to mention that earlier the air raid sirens went off. I had to call Edna to find out what to do. She said to stay inside until the all-clear signal came. I heard a signal and decided to go out. There were few cars and few people.

19 February 1991

It was a very, very cold day. As I walked to school I observed the damage the fire had done the night before. The building was being guarded by the MP's. I stopped to take a picture. Needless to say it was the talk of the day. People came from all around to watch the blaze. It was said that the water pressure was so low that the water couldn't reach the second floor of the two-story building. It wasn't until the Korean firemen came that they got results. There were several stories as to how the fire started. Some said there was an explosion, others said there was a gas leakage or an electrical shortage. The place was gutted. I was told that a few file cabinets were salvaged.

Fred acted like a fool again today. He brought in a final draft of his report and it was quite obvious that his mother had written it.

I went to observe Edna teaching at 11 o'clock. She didn't have the spunk that she had in November. I guess everyone was winding down. She came to watch me teach math in the afternoon.

I checked my mailbox and found a lovely Valentine's Day card from Gerald and a letter.

After school I went to the high school to try to get certificates printed for our training session. Mr. Muell who does the high school news paper, told me to come back next week and he would show me how to make them on the computer.

I came home because it was still very cold and that is where I have stayed.

20 February 1991

I awoke to a very cold morning. It started snowing about 12:30 p.m., just after lunch. It dumped a couple of inches. The sun came out and melted some of it before it turned cold again. We fear there will be freezing tonight.

I read today about the funeral of Reverend James Cleveland. He impacted many, composing hundreds of songs and having a gospel workshop of over 20,000 members worldwide.

21 February 1991

Schools were closed due to hazardous road conditions. The Lord knew that I needed a break. The teachers were told to come in when they could. Rosa was supposed to observe me teach. This was the second cancellation.

I went to school and worked awhile, then went to breakfast with Selena. I just had a cup of coffee. I worked longer in my room, then went shopping with Edna to buy Joyce's birthday gift. I bought her a purse and myself a top. I received a lovely Valentine's Day card from Tia and a letter from Beth. She said that Marian had to go into the hospital and that Jenny was going to Johns Hopkins Hospital for treatment for her eyes.

22 February 1991

This day is George Washington's birthday. It is also a very cold day. It is Colonial Day for the fifth graders. The children have filed in. Fred, too. He began by poking fun at the children in their colonial dress. Then he decided to punch Ryan. I wrote up a discipline record and sent him to Rosa Ridgely's office. She, in turn, called me to let me know that she was putting Fred on in-school suspension which meant I had to get work for him while he sat in a first grade class. The morning went well. At lunch time our apple juice was missing. We found it in Mary Canty's room. Sarah kept bugging me about giving her schoolwork because she would not be in school on Monday and Tuesday. AFKN (Air Force Korea Network), the T.V. station, came to tape us for the news. I wore a long black skirt, a black and white striped blouse, my black shawl and a cap a parent in the States bought for me in Williamsburg.

I returned home and wrapped Joyce's gift which was a Liz Claiborne handbag. It was now 8:10 p.m. and I turned in for the night.

The phone rang at 2:30 a.m. Whenever it does, I know that it is a call from the States from someone who has the time mixed up. It was Gerald. I was so happy to hear from him. Praise God.

He was at home. He said he worked for nine hours, so he could get every Friday off. He said things were going well. Patty, his girlfriend, planned to visit him in May. It was good hearing his voice.

23 February 1991

After Gerald called I went back to sleep and slept until 9:30 a.m., almost 7 hours. I had breakfast, went to the post office to mail Joyce's birthday gift. This was another cold day.

I returned home, ate an apple, a boiled egg and drank some juice. I had to catch the post bus to calligraphy class since I couldn't reach Edna. She arrived at class about 1:45 p.m. The instructor left us with our assignments to do because he had to go to a wedding at South Post chapel. I sat beside a Korean woman who was popping gum, so I moved.

I returned home, picked up some schoolwork and went to school for about a half hour. I returned home, read the paper and wrote Kenneth, my nephew, a letter. I rested, then prepared to go to the Performing Arts Center to see *Purlie*. It was great and quite a turnout for such a cold night. I photographed members of the cast and got their autographs.

24 February 1991

I decided to go to Main Post chapel. The music, prayer and sermon were great. I placed Jenny's name on the prayer request slip for her eyesight. The deacon prayed for her in the service. I didn't give her name but I asked that a prayer be offered for my sister's vision. I placed a prayer request for Gerald at South Post chapel and Main Post chapel and the prayers were answered in full. I believe in miracles.

This afternoon I went to the 8th Army Concert at Moyer Recreation Center. The program featured music by black composers and it was fantastic. There were six brothers in the band. Almost half of the *Purlie* cast was there.

I returned home and had a light meal. Flowers called. He said he would call back later or stop by.

The news was on. The ground war had stopped. It was a critical time for all of us.

25 February 1991

Rosa came to do a formal observation of me. The children were great! She stayed for thirty minutes. Later in the day I had a conference with her and she expressed how pleased she was with my lesson. She rated me "Excellent"! She was impressed with the fact that I was teaching the children how to do a research paper complete with note taking, outlining, drafts and the finished paper. Parents helped out and were excited, too.

I held my 11th calligraphy class, went home and relaxed.

26 February 1991

It is a little warmer. I prepared a finger platter of cucumbers, carrots, deviled eggs, and tomatoes for our faculty meeting. Someone came up with the idea of serving food at faculty meetings which are held every month. Teachers sign up to bring food each month.

I stopped at my classroom to drop off some work and to put the platter in the refrigerator, then waited for the post bus to take me to the hospital. There are mostly servicemen aboard this time of the day. I arrived there at 8:10 a.m. My appointment was for 8:45 a.m. The receptionist took me right away. I was told to go to the next room, change into a gown and come back to the laboratory. I questioned that. I would have to pass by a waiting room to get to a restroom to change into a gown, come back through the waiting room with mostly males, and pass the door and the office to the laboratory in a gown. So the receptionist said, "You can change in the lab. Many people complain about that arrangement, but we share the restrooms/dressing room with the adjacent clinic."

The technician took several x-rays. I was out at 8:45 a.m. I went to Family Clinic to weigh myself and to get my blood pressure checked. I then went to get my prescriptions refilled which included multiple vitamins. Afterwards, I decided to walk home because the weather was nice and I needed the exercise. (It was about 9:15 a.m.) As I approached home, I could see my class walking to music class.

After work we had a staff meeting which lasted until 3:35 p.m. The food was great. I went back to my classroom to prepare for the next day. I came home exhausted.

27 February 1991

The district superintendent's office which caught fire was razed this morning. Ben thought he was going to spend the day at the window watching it. After school I went to the high school where Mr. Mueller showed me how to print certificates on the computer.

I've learned that to succeed in life one needs goals and alternatives. One always should work and operate with two or more plans in mind. Never depend on one person or situation entirely. If you do, you will often be disappointed. You never know what people have in mind, even your so-called friends. Secretly, they can be envying and plotting against you. One must be watchful of men who dislike women who are making better progress and more money than men. Each night I review the day's actions and plan for tomorrow. I always say to myself, "I am going to do it this way, but if that doesn't work, I'll have to do so and so." I think hard about how I accomplish what I set out to do, and I can always find a way to do it. I've learned not to boast or brag about my success, but be thankful for it. Let others brag. I've also learned to encourage myself.

I've learned to try to do what I've set out to do. It is never too late to start over. If one thing fails, I keep trying. I looked and prayed for a better place to work and I found one. So far, so good- a job with numerous opportunities. I've learned to keep in prayer.

28 February 1991

This is the last day of the month. I wore a jacket to school, but it turned out to be colder than I thought. Mrs. Knoy, my principal, came in to observe a lesson on sedimentary rock and the breaking down of rock. Mrs. Knoy arrived at 10:55 a.m. and stayed until 11:40 a.m. The lesson went well. Fred had to be silly as usual. I had to threaten Ben and Vince with my eyes.

At 2:15 p.m. I went to Beatrice Knoy's office for a follow-up conference. She was quite impressed with my teaching. She said I reminded her of herself as a teacher. She asked if I had taken the STT course. She said she noticed I had momentum, and that I used cues, wait time and forewarning. I mentioned to her that I was interested in the art teacher position and the TAG position. She made a note of it.

I rushed to Sandy Corner's room for the science fair meeting. Her room was so impressive. She had a lot of Eastern art. She offered to take me to Main Post after the meeting, but she took so long that I hopped a ride with Edna. It was payday for all the military, so the line was *wrapped* around the building.

I was just relaxing at home when Selena came by. She wanted to see the dress the sewing lady had made. She left at 6:15 p.m., so I rushed to get dressed to go to the high school to see a presentation on Black History Month. My friends, Ellen Mead and Diane Johnson, were the sponsors so I wanted to be there to support them. The program lasted from six-thirty to seven.

1 March 1991

March came in like a lamb, a little cool, but nice. The day went fine. Sarah, a Korean child, came in loaded down with Girl Scout cookies. I purchased a box. Later in the morning we had a spelling bee. There were three winners, but I had only two prizes, so I had to give the third winner my box of cookies as a prize. I later looked in my desk drawer and found another prize, a fun book. I asked Tanya if she would rather have the fun book instead of the cookies. She said, "No." I wanted my cookies back. Well, I checked my weight later and found I had lost a pound, so I was glad I had given the cookies away.

Ten teachers were notified that they had received transfers to go to other places such as Germany, Iceland, the Philippines, Okinawa, etc. They were shouting for joy!!

That evening I went with Kathy, Carolyn and Bill to Harvey Aler's wedding reception in Riverside Apartments. These apartments are located outside the base. We had some difficulty finding them and so did everyone else. It was a lovely affair. There was plenty of food and drinks. The music which was from the 50's was even nice. Many of the staff members were there.

Mary Canty, who taught in the class next to mine was there. Mary always wore pants or long skirts. Tonight she had on a dress that had a hemline above her knees. I can understand why she wore pants so much. She had *teacher legs*. In other words *pencil legs*. Tiny-y-y-y!!!

I met a fellow there who was an electrical engineer. He

was contracted by Texas Instruments to work in Yongsan. We talked at length and exchanged phone numbers.

We arrived back at base at about 10 p.m. The 6 p.m. to 6 a.m. curfew was on, but we were able to get back on base.

2 March 1991

This was the day that Amira, my niece was to wed. I called to wish her well and goofed on the time. I reached John, her father at 3:15 a.m. Of course, Marian was all ready to talk, but I made it a brief conversation.

I awoke later, checked papers and reviewed my talk for the training session next Saturday. I then went over to Main Post to board the bus going to Panmunjon at the 38th Parallel in the Demilitarized Zone. It was quite a tour. We were given such strict directions and I was a little scared at first but I kept my composure. We stopped first at Camp Bonifas for lunch. Camp Bonifas was named for the soldier who was hacked to death by a North Korean guard while Bonifas was trimming a poplar tree so that the Americans could have a clearer view of the North Korean station. There is a plaque where the tree stood. We passed through Freedom Village on the south side and saw Propaganda Village on the north side.

We went up in the Freedom Tower to get a clear view of the north side of Korea. We then went into the room where negotiations were held. There was a table with a microphone wire running down the middle of the table. The wire separates the north side from the south side of Korea. We then went to an area where we saw signs placed every 10 meters to identify the demarcation line at the Bridge of No Return and Freedom Bridge. We also saw the flag pole displaying the largest flag in the world (30 meters wide).

I had my name engraved on a key chain with a cast of the Freedom Tower on the other side. I also purchased a certificate which stated that I had entered the demilitarized zone. I had our guide, Specialist Friedland, fill it in for me.

We then returned to Seoul at about 5:10 p.m.

I rested. At about 9:30 p.m. I went to Valerie Winston's house for a party. Valerie is one of the school's secretaries. She and her husband will be returning to the States in May. The Army movers are coming to pick up their furniture on Tuesday so they wanted to have a farewell party prior to that. The party was great. Good music, good food, good drinks. I danced several times. Rosa was there wearing jeans and dancing wildly. When she would get up to dance the guys would make wolf calls. At one point she said that when she dances she sweats. So the guys started yelling "Make her sweat, Ray. Make her sweat, man."

We left about 1:30 a.m.

3 March 1991

After church service, Tammi's husband and children met me at school to take me home to change my clothes. I was going to spend the afternoon with them.

I went to their house which is located in Dong Bronze Power. We were later joined by Leo and Cindy Rodriguez. They are from New Mexico. We chatted, then went for a tour of the neighborhood. It was great being a part of the daily activities of the people of Korea. I went to a typical Korean supermarket and bought some things and to a book center to purchase some Korean stationery. I also went into a Korean florist shop where I purchased a plant. Tammi's ceilings are covered with wood tile. The floors are also tiled. Traditional Korean homes do not have closets. Koreans have pipes that run beneath the floor to provide heat and water has to be heated by plugging in a cord. They had to buy distilled water for drinking and cooking.

I returned to Tammi's house where we had a dinner of salad, rice, beef stew and macaroni and cheese. Cindy made strawberry cake with a nut icing. After eating we went to the rooftop which offered an excellent view of Seoul. We could see houses on the hillside on one side, the army base on another and the Han River on a third side. The rooftop was very spacious and offered a great breeze.

We returned to the house when I indicated that I would be leaving. Tammi drove me home and she went to the school to do some work.

Before going to bed, I read the first chapter in Luke. Luke 1:37 says, "Nothing is ever impossible with God." That was the comforting message that I needed. I know that God can work Gerald's financial situation out and that He can perform a miracle for Jenny if they would believe that He could. I find so much comfort in reading the Bible when I am depressed and troubled. I would encourage anyone to do the same. I keep a copy of the New Testament and Psalms and Proverbs in my purse always.

The superintendent's building that was burned has been torn down and leveled. I heard that they are going to make the grounds into a park. The Koreans are hard workers and they did a fine and quick job of cleaning up the area. They are now in the process of building a stone wall on the base. It is amazing how they work.

4 March 1991

Today was a busy day. I sent interim reports home on Friday. I will have a conference with Fred's mother on Tuesday and with Vince's parents on Wednesday. Fred talked constantly and cried when I reprimanded him. If he wasn't talking, he was sleeping. The school psychologist came in to talk to the class and Fred's conduct was such that she had to tell the class to ignore him.

After school I had bus duty and then I had to rush back to my calligraphy group. A military father came in with his daughter who was crying. She said she no longer wanted to be in my calligraphy class because it was boring. He was angry with her because he said she was not mature enough to tell me.

5 March 1991

It was a very pleasant day weatherwise. Things went well. After school I had to attend a meeting on how to administer the California Test of Basic Skills. Then I met with the Nevens to discuss Fred's progress. I went home to drop off my things.

When I left work, I couldn't lock my classroom door. The maintenance man took the lock off last Thursday and replaced it, but it still doesn't work. The doorknob has come off about seven times this school year.

I went up to Hartell House to get some won, then over to Dragon Hill Lodge to price a party tray for Saturday's training session.

I will spend the rest of the evening at home. It is quite warm in my apartment.

6 March 1991

The weatherman predicted that the temperature would be 50-60 degrees, but it didn't feel like it. The day went okay. Ryan's mother sent a note stating that three of my children ruined a piece of artwork that her son was working on and that they had been teasing him for a month. She also called Nancy Nelson, the art teacher, and Sandy Lemons, the counselor. Fred wasn't named initially but somehow became involved.

I had to meet with the Millos' regarding their son's performance in math. I had to refer him to the math resource teacher. Mrs. Millo brought a stack of papers to show me how she had been working with her son. She said the math teacher didn't help him at all. After reassessing the conference when she left, I couldn't quite figure out why she had come to school except to show me how she was helping her son in math. Her husband is an elderly man who sat silently throughout the meeting. He told me at the end of the meeting that he is the quiet one. His wife runs the house, but they are very much interested in their son's performance at school. They are from Guam.

I had to report to maintenance that I couldn't lock my door. The custodian claimed he changed the lock the night before.

I had to go to the main building to meet with Amy to finish planning the training session for Saturday. I then went to Townhouse to put in an order for a party tray for lunch on Saturday.

I returned to school, checked papers and filled out my civilian travel papers. I plan to leave Korea on June 15th, the day after school closes and spend four days with Gerald in California before going home.

7 March 1991

The day was a brisk one. It was also Joyce's birthday. Fred was out to a special class just about all morning.

Yesterday, when I left school, I couldn't lock my door. This morning I couldn't open it. It had been nailed from the inside and the maintenance man had not come in. I arrived at school at 7 a.m. and couldn't get into my room until 7:35 a.m. Besides that, I couldn't find my folder with Saturday's training information. I was really upset, but I later found it packed away with my other materials.

We wrote notes to send home for parents to make items for our bake sale next week. We also started making posters. The day before, my children made molars, three layered construction paper pictures. Since they turned out nicely, I displayed all of them.

8 March 1991

The day started off as a very cold rainy one and later turned into a slushy snowy one. The children were quite hyperactive. The day got off to a bad start. I went to work and found my door nailed closed on the inside. The other two teachers hadn't come in so I couldn't go through their rooms to enter mine. Mr. Benden wasn't in and no one in the office had a master key. My doorknob had come off approximately seven times this year. For the past week I couldn't lock my door, so I went to the principal to complain. I was cold, wet and laden down with school materials.

At lunch time, the children were sent back to my room five minutes early. So I went dashing up to Mr. Pike, the assistant principal, who was in the cafeteria and complained. The children had been *hell* all morning. The MP dog demonstration had been canceled because of the weather. Crystal Canty, the complaining child in my class, passed out invitations for a surprise birthday slumber party which I thought was strange because her birthday was in December and she knew about this party, so it wasn't a surprise. I didn't bother to ask her. The afternoon wore on. At the end of the day I had three boys help me deliver training seminar materials to the main building, then I met with Amy and Brianne to finalize plans for the training seminar and to set up the room.

It was still snowing and slushy.

9 March 1991

Today our minority training workshop is being held. The weather is rather warm, luckily, so the snow that fell didn't freeze.

It was only slushy. Heaven was with me. I was the first to arrive at school for the training session. Edna had been working in her room since 7 a.m. We set up and got started about 9:20 a.m. Everything went very well. We had thirteen participants and three presenters. At the end of the session we awarded certificates. I penned in the names in calligraphy. We passed out evaluation forms. At the bottom was a rating scale of one to twelve. The ratings fell between ten and twelve except one that was seven which fell between fair and good. There were several positive comments on my presentation on leadership involvement. We ended our session an hour early.

10 March 1991

I was debating how I would go to church, attend ceramic class and go to Chloe's for a grade level meeting with such a tight schedule. So I decided not to go to church. I took my walk and returned home to go to my ceramic class only to find out that the class was canceled, so I returned home.

I tried to decide on a short trip for my spring break. I was very much impressed with my visit to Singapore, which is very beautiful, and clean. I just read that there is a $500.00 fine for spitting in Singapore. Koreans spit a lot, so they are trying to crack down on it as well as crack down on violence and crime.

Dora came over and we got a cab to Chloe Macklin's for a grade level meeting. Debbie, Dolly, Mary and Judy were already there. We had drinks, snacks and veggies as we discussed school in general and our rummage sale in particular. We then had a meal of salad, lasagna and toasted french bread and more drinks. Afterwards we discussed our camping trip, then had dessert which consisted of a fruit cup, angel food cake and more drinks. It was nearing 7 p.m. and Dora had to get home because her husband had to go out in the field.

In March, Korea has what is called Team Spirit which is when Korea and the U.S. check their preparedness for war which involves some combat simulation. It was said that North Korea is a hot spot.

11 March 1991

Today was a little different. I was able, however, to open and lock my door. We gave the children a standardized test, the California Test of Basic Skills (CTBS). I gave mine in the morning. The children then went to art. Afterwards the school psychologist came in to talk to the class. After lunch I took the class around the campus to put up our bake sale posters.

I held my 13th calligraphy club training. I had one fourth grader who had made tremendous strides. I had another child who was excellent also and there were a few more. I only had one boy in my sessions.

12 March 1991

The children didn't have to come to school. We attended a math workshop at school. The workshop ended at 2:30 p.m. Selena and I had nothing to do so we hung out. We went to Gate 19, Selena shopped, I didn't. From there we went to the Navy Club, but it was under renovation, so we went to Oasis in Dragon Hill Lodge for enchiladas. We then went to the bookstore in Dragon Hill and sat in the lounge awhile. Selena kept running into all of the men she knew. I came home to do some schoolwork and to study for the N.T.E.

13 March 1991

I asked the secretary to cut orders for me to go to Okinawa, Japan for my spring break. If I can get a military flight I will only have to pay $10.00. I could stay in a BOQ like the one I live in free or at least at little cost. All of us are beginning to count our money. We have three months more to work and we won't get paid during the summer. I am trying to get a Korean student or students to teach English. That is big business and pays well.

It is Friday, the end of another long week. The day was a very busy one. I gave three of the 10 CTBS tests. We also had our bake sale. Four parents helped out, including Danielle Canty, Crystal's mom. We made $111.65. If we had not run out of baked foods, we could have made about $50.00 more if everyone had contributed. About seven or eight children did not.

14 March 1991

Although I took the day off so that I can take the N.T.E., I still went to school to get the class started on the CTBS. Luckily, I did because the substitute didn't show up until a few minutes past 8 a.m. I got the class started on the tests.

I went to Main Post to pick up a receipt showing I had paid for a platter of food for the training session. I needed it to be reimbursed. I then went to the Education Center to take the test. I took this test twenty-seven years ago, but the Education Testing Service in Princeton, N.J. does not report test results after twenty years, so I had to pay $70.00 to take the test again. The first part lasted for two hours. We were given a lunch break. The next part of the test lasted two hours. My brain was dead tired. For each session, it took half an hour to fill in the information blocks.

I came home and changed quickly to go to Hartell House for a Mexican festival meal. It was delicious and all you can eat for $8.50.

15 March 1991

We went to Taegu, Korea, for a teachers association meeting. I went to Betsy Rollin's to get a ride to Moyer Recreation Center where we got a taxi to go to Seoul Station to board the train for Taegu. It was raining mixed with snow. The station was crowded as usual. We met with Ella Mead, then Pat Class, Sharon Reed and Pat Goins. When we boarded the train, Nancy Nelson, Judy Richard, Hattie Higg, Amy Smart, Pam

Garberine and a host of other T.E.A.K. members were already on. We rode for about half an hour before we started distributing food. Each person brought food for a meal on the train. We arrived in Taegu at about 11 a.m. and took a taxi to Camp George and to the school where we were to meet. The meeting went well. I gave my report on our MIP Training Seminar. I brought along some of the flyers we had left over from the training.

16 March 1991

I awakened about 7 o'clock, took a shower and got ready to go to breakfast at Camp Walker. We took a cab there. Service didn't start until 11 a.m., so we did a little shopping in the PX. We went to Protestant Service which was nice and quiet, quite like the service at South Post chapel.

We arrived at the train station about 1:25 p.m. A Korean girl with grey eyes approached me saying that Christ Jesus has arisen and is alive. She acted very strange. Koreans were looking at her. She came upstairs to the restaurant where we were still saying, "Jesus is risen." She sat down and lit a cigarette. She walked about and took another seat. Koreans in the train station were staring at us as well as at her.

We ate junk food all the way back to Seoul, Korea.

Back in Seoul, we went to Oriental Gardens for dinner. I ordered chicken fried rice. I had ordered beef fried rice the day before in Taegu.

17 March 1991

Tavia called me to inform me that she was no longer employed. Heaven help us all. I know things have not gone well for her and this concerned me a great deal. She is a hard worker and is very loving and caring. I cannot say that life has not been good to her because it has, but one must be good to oneself in more than material things. One has to step back and look at his life and himself and take an assessment. Why are these things happening to me? What can I do about my life? Should I take a new approach to my thinking, the way I relate to people, the way I carry myself, my behavior? What is it that I'm striving for? What are my goals? How can I reach them? Should I go beyond my physical environment? Should I meet different people? Engage in other activities? Limit my spending?

I'm hoping that I can impact more on Tavia's life so that it will be less stressful, but one has to decide for himself that he is going to make things better for himself, and with God's help, he will overcome for there is no failure in God.

18 March 1991

We have to work nine more days until spring break. The morning was quite cool, and pleasant. The children were as noisy this morning as they were on Friday so I had each to write a composition titled, "Why I Should Not Talk While My Teacher is Talking." They did a fine job of writing, but did they follow through? No! The school psychologist came in and told them that they were the noisiest and wildest of the fifth grade classes she has worked with.

After school, I had my 14th calligraphy class. My students practiced a letter style of their choice, then wrote a few famous words on parchment. I explained to them about the making, use and history of parchment.

I thought about Tavia's situation with her job. I knew she would find something. I was hoping that she would strive to make her life more comfortable. Perhaps when I return home we can do more things together.

19 March 1991

I thought about Tavia. With effort she can have the administrator's position. She has the know-how, but she must work on herself by aligning herself with people who are going somewhere in life. She must surround herself with upwardly mobile, positive thinking, strong and supportive people and friends. One must also guard his conversation and plans. Never let everyone know what you are doing and what you are thinking. People can stifle you if they are envious.

This was a beautiful day weatherwise. Fred fell asleep after two weeks of abstaining.

Tony called last night and said he would call again between 7 and 8 p.m. I probably won't answer the phone.

20 March 1991

Spring was supposed to have come in at 10 a.m. this morning. The day went well until 10:30 a.m. when we went to the library. Ms. Fearson, the army band leader's wife, steamed off at Fred. She said he snatched a book and that was the final straw. She said she wasn't paid enough money to put up with him, so she went storming off to Rosa Ridgely's office to report his behavior. Rosa sent for Fred. When I returned to my class, Rosa called, wanting to discuss Fred. She had called Fred's mother. This child has caused me more problems than the entire class.

After school I went to aerobics class in the school's Dolphin Theater. We performed to a video which was an hour long. I survived. I could stand to lose some weight.

I left school and went to Oriental Gardens for dinner. I sat in the bar area until dark so I could take a picture of the Seoul Tower overlooking the city.

21 March 1991

This was the first full day of spring. There was a sort of chill in the air. I look forward to a nice day. I would do little teaching today. Amy Smart, the language arts specialist, came to teach the class for forty minutes. In the afternoon we were going to watch *Square One,* a math show on T.V. and then go to the research library to research great women for National Women's History Month. The day was almost ruined when Jo Kim decided to lock Ryan Hend's head in his arm. Fred and Jeremy were a part of this action also. I wrote up a discipline report and sent them off to Rosa Ridgely's office.

Edna brought me a nice big salad that would last for two days. She said she was going to help me lose weight. I decided, in my shopping, I will purchase mostly fruits, vegetables and fish.

22 March 1991

Friday at last!!! *Reading Rainbow,* a reading show, was not transmitted through the school's closed circuit T.V. because Russ Corb and Mickey Fellon, workers in the Media Center, were absent.

I took the class to the library to take notes for their research papers. Our library is a sorry one and so is our librarian, Mrs. Patterson. There is a rumor that next year will be her last year.

Dora and her husband picked me up to go to a *hen* party. Jacquie Youngston, the music teacher, had a birthday and she wanted to celebrate. Her husband was away at Team Spirit so I guess she didn't want to have any men guests.

Earlier in the day, Selena gave me a seven-day diet that I try. I had seen it before. The first day you eat all fruit. The second day, vegetables, preferably green leafy ones. The third day, fruit and vegetables. The fourth day, bananas and skim milk. The fifth day, beef and tomatoes. The sixth day, beef and vegetables, and the seventh day, brown rice, unsweetened fruit and vegetables. You should lose 10-17 pounds. I will give it a try.

23 March 1991

I woke up with two things on my mind; Tavia and my diet. I called Tavia and found out that things were okay. She is dealing with her situation. I thought I would attempt my diet with this first day. Day one I ate all fruit, but no bananas. I violated the first day! I ate cold cereal for breakfast. I drank a diet Coke and later some tomato juice.

I went to Main Post to meet with Carolyn Brow to board the bus to Camp Carey. The bus was very crowded with mostly black men and women. The ride was about two hours long and some passengers had to stand. Camp Carey was quite busy, the opposite of Camp Henry at Taegu last week. We had a light lunch at the Gateway Club on base. We then went out the gate to the streets to do some shopping. I only purchased a top to match my khaki pants. What was unusual about these shops is that the names are written in English. It was like being in the States. We returned to Camp Carey and again the bus was very crowded. I had to stand as well as others until we reached Camp Red Cloud where several people alighted.

We arrived at the base at 7 p.m. I called Selena and chatted for awhile. I then called Vince who had been trying to contact me all week. We talked at length.

Rob and Selena picked me up at about 9:45 to go to Calvin Thomas' promotion party. The usual people were there. There was the usual food and usual music. It was some place to go. "I was thinking, I have never partied this much in one year as I have here." It has been exciting. I brought some birthday cake home. There goes the diet.

24 March 1991

I awakened at about 7 a.m., had breakfast, read the paper and prepared to go to South Post chapel. My schedule was tight. Service was beautiful! A young group known as "Continental" came from the States to minister "the word" in song. It was also Palm Sunday. The palms we received were quite different from the ones we get in the States in that they were whole leaves instead of a strip.

After service I went to Main Post to Moyer Recreation Center to make a two piece ceramic canister. It took about two and a half hours. From there I walked down the hall to the auditorium for the 8th Army Band Concert. They performed well as usual. The band had six men participating. One, Officer Seay, was very good. He had even arranged a song. When I arrived, Edna was already there. We were later joined by her friend, a gentleman she met at church.

25 March 1991

I removed Fred from the room again. He insisted on trying to catch a fly while I was teaching. At my break time the assistant principal suggested that I refer him to the school psychologist. The special education teacher sent for him at 1:15.

I held my 15th calligraphy class. At this point, the pupils are at different stages in their performance. They are making borders, writing on parchment and personalizing a folder.

I went from calligraphy club to aerobic class. There were only six of us in this session.

26 March 1991

I dressed lightly because I thought it would be warm, but it turned out to be a typical chilly, windy March day. I dressed up because we were to have a class picture taken. I was disappointed that after telling my class everyday for a week that pictures were to be taken, only about eight or nine looked decent. The rest looked like ragamuffins. They looked the worst that I have ever seen them. Despite that, a little joy came into my day. Fred came in and announced that his mother would be picking him up to go to be tested ALL DAY!!! She came in about a half hour later to get him. She needed to be tested too!!! They came back at lunch time to get his things.

After school, we had a staff meeting. Members signed up to bring goodies and there were plenty. When I arrived in the media center there was a group of six of my girl students coming to work on their research papers. Mr. Corb showed them the door. I had given them time in the library last week to find information but they spent the time socializing.

The superintendent's office which was destroyed by fire has been torn down. They will make a park where the building once stood.

27 March 1991

This was another chilly day. Nothing special happened. Fred continued to act like a fool. I gave the children the 3rd unit reading test. I spent every free moment working on my report cards.

Crystal's mother approached me about her daughter's report. Crystal claimed she didn't know when it was due. I was in the library when she came to me. Fred was sitting at the table ASLEEP! I took the opportunity to snap his picture. Crystal's mother sympathized with him saying "Poor Fred, you'll make it." He said he had gone to the movies the night before.

After school, I changed into my jogging suit for my exercise session but it was canceled since so many people had other things to do and so did I. I went to Main Post to the bank, the post office and to Moyer to pick up my ceramic canister set. The walk over was my exercise. I returned home, had a light supper and worked on my report cards.

I am thinking that everywhere I move, from Baltimore to Washington, to Virginia, to Korea, I am always befriended by someone who would support me and stand by me. That is why I'm not afraid to venture out. I know that God will provide what I need.

28 March 1991

The day started off as a very warm day, but the temperature began to drop after 4 p.m.

I was tense all day. I didn't want anything to go wrong. You see, I planned to leave right after school to go to Osan Air Base to get a flight to Okinawa. I took my luggage to school and was transported to Osan in the Kings' van.

I was out of school at 2 p.m. with my luggage and at the van at 2:05 p.m. The Kings were there and we were off to Osan Air Base. We signed up for a flight to Okinawa where our names were placed in the computer to be called the next day if space was available. Carolyn Brow and Kathy Jannis arrived on the 4:30 p.m. bus.

We couldn't get a flight out so we went to our rooms to rest awhile then went over to La Contina Mexican Restaurant for dinner. We then returned to our rooms for the night. The rooms were very nice except they were extremely warm. I didn't sleep very well.

29 March 1991

I awakened about 5 a.m., got dressed and went over to Carolyn's about 6:15. She and Kathy weren't quite ready. In about 20 minutes we called a cab to take us to the MAC (Military Airlift Carrier). We got there about 6:45, had breakfast in the snack bar, then checked on our flight. While waiting, Selena and Rob came in. Selena said she couldn't find me yesterday to give me a ride. I didn't feel comfortable with her and Rob anyway. I was the third party tagging along.

We couldn't get the 12:05 flight out because it was carrying dangerous material. There was another flight out at 2:30 but I couldn't carry more than 30 pounds. I had Tavia's heavy Samsonite luggage. The total weight was 41 pounds. It so happened that Tammi had a lightweight nylon piece of luggage in her van that she allowed me to use. It was nice, but clumsy to handle. I weighed it along with my handbag and it weighed 28.4 pounds.

The announcer said that I could get on the C/2 flight. I was the only one out of the ten who was able to go to Okinawa, Japan, that day. Luckily, a teacher who was in my Study of Teaching Class and her husband were going to Okinawa so I didn't feel alone.

There were only seven of us on this flight because that was the plane's capacity. It reminded me of the crop duster that I flew in from Roanoke, Virginia to Raleigh, North Carolina. Four of us sat on one side and three on the other. The aisle was about a foot wide. There was, however, a toilet aboard. There were two pilots, an older man and a younger one. I took a picture with the co-pilot. The three hour flight was great.

I arrived at Kadena Base in Okinawa, Japan at 6 p.m. I checked in, then went to Japanese customs. From there I went to billeting. I had to go back to the terminal to register for a return flight. The flight only cost $10.00. I returned and had a light salad supper with my teacher friend and her husband.

30 March 1997

It was a year ago that I was notified that a position was being offered to me in DODDS. Little did I know what was in store for me.

I awakened about 6 o'clock this morning, showered and read. It was raining hard. I went to the officers club for breakfast which consisted of ham omelet, grits, toast, coffee and grapefruit juice. The coordinator of science for the Pacific region was there. I thought I recognized him. We chatted for a little while.

I left and went to billeting to pay for another night. The cost was $8.50. From there I went to the USO Club. I just missed a tour, so I decided to do a little shopping. I went to the recreation center to see if I could catch a tour. It was quite a long walk in the rain. A Japanese woman who worked in the barber shop at the Officers' Club lent me her umbrella.

It is now 8:25 p.m. and I haven't heard from the other teachers.

31 March 1991

I woke up at 6 a.m. to a chilly rainy Easter morning. I did not go to chapel sunrise service because I was not sure where it was and I didn't want to be out roaming so early in the morning.

Japanese drive on the left-hand side here. The country is green, beautiful and clean. Each household, for the most part, has two cars.

I was going to the Officers' Club to get some yen but it wasn't open, so I continued to Shogun Inn to pay for the day's billeting ($8.50). I checked to see if any of my co-workers from Seoul had arrived. They hadn't, so I went to Shilling Center to board the bus for a tour of Okinawa. The cost was $15.00. The tour guide allowed me to buy some yen from her. The yen value was 135 to $1.00 of our money. The tour guide was quite informative. We toured many monuments, temples, burial grounds, museums, and the cliff where numerous Japanese committed suicide. The battle of Okinawa was a very crucial one. I purchased a book on the battle to read more about it. We stopped for lunch at a typical Japanese restaurant. I ordered *soba,* a large bowl of noodles, with vegetables and bits of meat served with tea at a cost of 50 yen. I went next door to the super market which was neat and well stocked.

We arrived back at base about 4 p.m. I called Mia Hunter, a teacher at Okinawa. She said she would pick me up. After waiting a while I then called to see if she was coming. She said she had company and sent a friend named Pat to pick me up. When Pat didn't show I opened up a can of soda, drank it, put my bed clothes on and went to bed. About 11:30 p.m. Mia came. She said, "Get dressed we're going." It turned out Pat couldn't find the place. We went to the NCO Club which reminded me of Bentley's in Seoul, but larger with a live rap band. I was about to fall on my face because I was tired from the day-long walking tour. We left the club about 1 a.m. Pat drove me to my V.O.Q. (Visitor Officers' Quarters).

1 April 1991

It is April Fool's day and I am in my fourth day of tour on the island of Okinawa. I awakened, showered in cool water, ate breakfast, and went to the Officers' Club to get some yen and to call Mia Hunter.

I went to Shogun Inn to pay for billeting for the night only to find that I had to check out of my room. Military personnel have priority in the rooms so I put my name on the waiting list. It is now 11 a.m. I was to meet Mia at 11:30. Check out time was 12 noon, so I rushed to my room, packed in twenty minutes and rushed to the Officers' Club to meet Mia. She came a few minutes later, took me to pick up my luggage to take to storage at Shogun Inn. From there we went to her apartment for lunch. She had a large beautiful apartment. She had been in Okinawa for four years and loved it. I could see why. She served me a delicious meal of ham, candied potatoes, macaroni and cheese, greens and banana nut bread with coffee. I was so blessed to have met her, such a delightful person. We scheduled a day long tour that took us first to Kadena Marina which has a lovely sea view, then on to Okinawa Folk village where we saw replicas of buildings and activities of Okinawan life. The people here are very friendly. We saw a snake show, marching boys, and hundreds of college students dressed in their black uniforms and white tennis shoes. The students were well disciplined. We saw a beautiful lake with mallards, and we observed Okinawan women cooking. I took a picture with the woman pressing sugar cane using the power of an ox and a man feeding a goat milk from a baby bottle. As we rode along the road parallel to the beach, we witnessed some magnificent sights. We went to Manza Cliffs and saw beauty to behold in the sea and ocean, bluffs and cliffs, beautiful blue green water and interesting rock formations.

It was very windy so I couldn't get very close to the edge. Warnings had been flashed across the television screen warning people to be careful and to avoid sea activities because of the high winds.

I had to praise God for allowing me to meet Mia and for allowing me to see the beauty in the earth that He has created. I thought of Jenny and her eyesight and continued to pray and ask others to pray for her failing vision. If only she could see such beauty. I believe in prayer and I believe in miracles. I thought of Tavia and Gerald and their financial situation and prayed that they could work things out so that they can know the joy that I know.

We went on to a glass factory and watched skillful artisans make lovely glass pitchers. We went into the shop to see the glass items for sale. There was a display of *Girl's Day,* a day celebrated in Okinawa. Replicas of the *shi shi* dogs were sold everywhere. These were placed at the entrance of homes and temples because they are believed to bring good luck and wealth. Also paper cranes are lucky items. We rode back along the lovely scenic route with its beautiful trees. Mia and I talked a lot and found we have a lot in common.

We went to the billeting office and as Heaven would have it, there was a room available to me.

2 April 1991

I have given up on my co-workers coming from Seoul/Osan. I assume that if they didn't get a flight to Okinawa that they got one to Yokota, Japan.

I met with Mia and Nancy, the two teachers from Okinawa at the Officers' Club. We rode to Botanical Gardens where I saw the most lovely flowers and trees in the world. There were giant palms, king palms, bottle palms, powder puffs, and many types of plants. Some were unusual, too. The most striking feature was a large number of huge gold fish and carp. What the visitors would do was to purchase packets of fish food from the vending machine, then throw the food to the fish. The fish would scramble in large numbers to eat it. I had to take pictures of such a sight.

We then went to Tori Beach which was overwhelming. We walked for about a mile up the beach collecting shells. I got a beautiful haul. After that we had a quick meal at the Seaman's Club. We took the shells to Mia's apartment to soak in chlorine and water. Prior to that we went to Mia's school, Bob Hope Elementary. While there I showed Mia how to do calligraphy. I was also able to interest her in keeping a journal.

We went on to the USO Club where we met Nancy to go to Four Seasons, a Japanese restaurant. The chef prepared our meal of Kohe steak at the table. Besides steak we were served cubed potatoes with green peppers and onions, rice, onion sprouts with spinach leaves and Japanese beer. I took a picture of the skillful chef.

We were getting tired and sleepy from walking on the beach so we paid and departed. One doesn't tip in Japanese restaurants.

3 April 1991

Today was warmer than yesterday. Mia came to pick me up at 10 a.m. We went to pick up Hattie Newton, another teacher. We went to the bank to get some yen, then went on to Naha, a little town to the north. We went to a place called Black Market Alley where I purchased a black blouse, a unique birthday card for Beth and a pair of shi-shi ceramic dogs. As I mentioned, the dogs are for wealth and good luck. We had lunch at the Seaman's Club and took a tour of Camp Kinser.

We came home and called MAC terminal at Kadena. There was no plane flying out of Korea until Saturday, so we signed up at Futemma where a plane was scheduled to leave at 7 a.m. the next morning.

I said good-bye to Nancy and checked into another room. Then Mia and I had a salad at the Officers' Club. She consented to send the items that I purchased to me by MPS (Military Postal Service), free of charge.

4 April 1991

I awakened about 4:22 a.m. because I needed to go to Futemma for a possible flight out to Korea. I called for a cab the night before and went outside at 5:10 to wait. The cab was supposed to come at 5:15. When it didn't show at 5:25 I called again. It was raining hard. I arrived at Futemma about 5:53 a.m. There was a military couple there with their two sons. The sons attended Seoul American High School. I decided not to inform them that I taught at Seoul American Elementary School. I was checked in and then about a half hour later I was told that the flight was going directly to Seoul and they couldn't clear us there. We could only be cleared at Osan. Such was the case with space available flights. I called Mia and she came to get me at about 11:45 a.m. and we had lunch at Tiki Pizza. I had my souvenirs wrapped and sent to Korea. It doesn't cost anything to ship from base to base.

From there we went back to the air terminal at 1:50 p.m. I sat in the terminal from that time until 11:45 p.m. that night waiting for a flight. During that time I read and read and read and watched T.V. That evening I went upstairs and ordered Yaki soba, a fried noodle with bits of meat, cabbage and carrot dish and a Coke. I changed clothes in the ladies room and put on another piece of jewelry. There were shower facilities for women on the second level.

Mia picked me up from the air terminal at 11:45 p.m. and we went to the NCO club for a disco. Although it was raining quite hard, there was a crowd there. Mia ordered a beer and I ordered a Coke. I was already getting sleepy so I didn't want to chance falling asleep after drinking a beer. I danced about three times to the long dance videos. I never danced so much before I left home. Surely I must have lost some weight. We left there about 12:55 a.m. I asked Mia if I could spend the night at her place. She had offered before. Mind you, I had been up twenty-one hours so I had no trouble getting to sleep.

5 April 1991

I awoke about 6 a.m. Mia was awake because she spoke as soon as I got up. She called terminals while I dressed. Kadena had nothing leaving for Korea until Saturday morning. There was one at Futemma with one seat available. I didn't want to chance going up there to be canceled again so we went to Kadena Air Terminal to wait. I called Yvonne Wingman about 8 p.m. She had just arrived last night from Seoul by way of a MAC flight. She said she had been trying to leave since Monday.

The *All Star Salute to Our Troops* was telecast over F.E.N.S. (Foreign Network) from Andrews Air Force Base. President and Mrs. Bush were in the audience. Among the guest performers were B.B. and C.C. Winans accompanied by the Eastern High School's choir directed by Joyce Garrett. I was so glad to see her that I took out my camera and took snapshots of her from the T.V. screen. Joyce is a member of my church. This was at 9:45 p.m. Yvonne Wingman and her friend, Sonny, took me to her house at 11 p.m.

6 April 1991

I awakened and got up at 4:30 a.m. thinking it was 5:30 a.m. I spent a very restful night at Yvonne's place which was off base. Like Nancy and Mia, she had a lovely apartment with a large collection of baskets and shells. She fixed me coffee and took me to the MAC terminal. It was raining again and the terminal was full. After checking in I had to go to immigration to be checked out of the country. This type of travel was yet another new experience for me. The aircraft had no windows and only a couple of port holes on either side. It was very noisy so we were given little yellow styrofoam earplugs. One could order a box lunch, but we were too late to order. The aircraft was rugged with pipes in the ceiling and steam coming from them, too. It was shaky. What an experience, but what could you say for $10.00. I said a prayer as we were lifting into the air.

It was now 8:40 a.m. and I was aboard a very noisy green military aircraft with Jane Stout and her husband. They were the couple who flew over with me.

It was now 10:45 a.m. and the plane touched down at Chinhae, Korea. The plane was opened wide from the rear and the crew was unloading a large wooden crate and some other cargo. The passengers were standing, stretching their legs. A Filipino lady whom I met in the terminal came over to chat with me. She worked in a hospital in Okinawa, but her husband was stationed at Kunsan, Korea (an air base). I was told that air force bases were in the States and air bases were overseas.

I told one of the crew that this was my first flight and that I'd like to take a picture. He said, "Sure, why don't you come up to the flight deck," and so I did. There were about 5 or 6 men on the pilot's deck. One took my picture sitting in the cockpit.

We touched down about noon, gained custom clearance and boarded an army bus for a three-hour ride to Osan Air Base where I boarded a bus for a two-hour ride to Seoul. Seoul is only 25 miles from Osan, but the road/highway is just so crowded. I got a cab, arrived at my BOQ and called Edna for my key. She brought it over and we chatted briefly.

7 April 1991

On the way to school, I noticed that several buildings had been painted a mustard/caramel color trimmed in brown. I intended to drop off a few things at work, but spent some time there working. I then went to check my mailbox. There were letters from Marian, Ada and a nice card from Gerald. He also sent me a copy of his performance evaluation. It was rated "SUPERIOR"! I jumped for joy and praised God. I knew he would do well. He had tried so hard at Virginia State University to succeed.

I called Tavia earlier, but she wasn't at home. Someone by the name of Debbie was baby-sitting for her. Tavia returned my call at midnight.

8 April 1991

This was the first day at work after spring break. It was a very busy day. Troll Books arrived, so I distributed them. I also had to distribute survey forms and information on our camping trip. I had the children to tell of anything interesting and exciting that they did over the spring break. Crystal Canty took a Space A hop to Yokota, Japan, which she didn't find interesting because they stayed in billeting. Brianne Yen went to Guam for a day and said it was so-so. Most of the others went to Lotte Amusement Park.

I checked the mailroom and my boxes from Okinawa were there, but I can't get them until tomorrow.

I had my 16th session with my calligraphy club. We spent the session finishing up projects we had started and practicing writing by using smaller letters.

I was too tired to go to aerobics. Speaking of being tired, Fred slept most of the day. The children said he did the same thing last year so the teacher gave up trying to keep him awake.

I had my children to begin to make the papier mache' mask forms for Friday's presentation to Nancy Benton's sixth graders.

When I got to work and, in fact, all weekend, people were saying to me, "So you're the lucky one. You were the only one of your group to get out to Okinawa."

9 April 1991

I couldn't believe it. I overslept this morning, but I got to work on time. I guess it was the glass of Burgundy I drank last night, the traveling last week, and my busy job.

Fred slept again today. He also ate rice crackers and brought a quart bottle of drink to school.

I checked my mailbox and I had four large boxes, three were from my trip to Okinawa and a fourth from Beth. She sent me some clothes. That was thoughtful of her.

I had every intention of going to work early today, but I had to clean my shells. I put some in a basket to put in the bathroom.

Today was a busy, but a fruitful day. The children were very excited because it was report card day. Fred tried to doze off again. I met with the team leader teacher, then went to my classroom to work. I came home to work on my shells and to do schoolwork.

11 April 1991

I arose early and arrived at school before 7 a.m. The day was busy but it went well. While Amy Smart taught my class, I slipped home to get my tie dyes and to have my cleaning lady iron my dress. Fred fell asleep again. This was the fourth time this week. We finished most of the mask forms today and painted them. I dried them with a fan.

After work I took my things to the Dolphin Theater so they would be there for the African mask presentation. Another teacher is having an assembly tomorrow. I hope it won't interfere with what I am doing.

12 April 1991

I had to make two trips to work to carry my things for my mask presentation. The morning was a busy one. There was so much to do, collect permission slips for the MP dog demonstration, the camping trip, collect survey forms, Troll Book order money and report card envelopes.

My African mask presentation was very good. The children enjoyed it. They didn't make nearly as much a mess as the other classes. I invited the assistant principal to my presentation. She said I should have informed her earlier so that she could have called the T.V. station. I didn't want that because this presentation was a dress rehearsal for my presentation to the teachers on Friday.

Fred fell asleep for the fifth time this week. I have a fine snapshot of him sleeping.

I checked my weight and found that I had lost two pounds.

13 April 1991

I awakened to a very damp morning. That meant that our fifth grade rummage sale and bazaar would be canceled, so I went to school and worked on the computer, training myself for about three hours. Then I went to the shoppette to get some vitamin E when I ran into Dora Johns and her husband, Battalion Commander Jeff Johns, who invited me to see *Purlie* again. I then took my daily walk which lasted for one hour.

I relaxed a little before preparing to go to see *Purlie*. Dora and her husband said that they wanted me to meet someone, but the person didn't show up. The show *Purlie* was even better than before. I took more snapshots of the cast.

14 April 1991

Edna invited me to go with her to a service at 121 Evacuation Hospital chapel at 9:30. It was a warm, quiet service with loving people, beautiful familiar music and an inspirational message. I left there and went to Memorial Gospel Service which was just the opposite. The Deltas were there dressed in their red and white, and the Land Prince Hall Masons dressed in white. It was a very emotional service. The young lady seated behind me was far along in her pregnancy and was not feeling well. She sent in a prayer request.

I took my one hour walk around South Post. My route was to walk down 8th Army Drive to Gate 19 back to Medical Loop, pass the hospital, pass Collier Field House, back up to 8th Army Drive to Stoves Road behind the school, to the road leading pass the Army Community Service building, to Corps Road through the housing development pass the golf course, to the main road in front of the school, to the road where I live.

I found out that the fellow Dora wanted me to meet had to return to Taegu, Korea.

The phone rang at about 12:25 a.m. It was Ned. I was so glad to hear his voice. He said among other things that he was going to send me the Bundu mask.

15 April 1991

Today is the deadline for filing income taxes in the U.S. and it was also Beth's birthday. I called her this morning to wish her a *Happy Birthday* but she was out with a friend. Stanley answered the phone. He realized that it was a costly call so he made his conversation short.

I had my seventeenth calligraphy class, three more to go!! We copied a poem in smaller print on parchment.

16 April 1991

It is less than two months before I will return home. The class was extremely quiet for about 50 minutes this morning. It was remarkable. At 9 a.m. we went to the outside of the main building to hear the Band of Wales play. They were outstanding.

We were having Korean artists-in-residence in our building. They too were super. They were working in pastels, block printing, water color and crayon.

After work Selena and I went to the transportation office to apply for our plane tickets home and then to another transportation office to make an appointment for shipping some of our things back home.

Fred fell asleep again today, so I wrote a note to the nurse who in turn called his pediatrician. He informed me that Fred was having a battery of tests and he had several problems that included being anemic. So rather than knock myself out, I moved his desk to a corner and I let him sleep whenever he wanted.

17 April 1991

I thought the day would go well, but that Fred Proctor would not stop talking so I could start my lesson, so I sent him to the office. Rosa called his mother. She said she sat in my class observing and other children were talking and I didn't put them out. I think she was confused because she has never sat in my room.

After work I went to the Chosun to buy four rice bowls. They had saucers from Hong Kong on sale, so I purchased some. It started to rain, so I couldn't take a walk. I went back to school to get Marcia Cain to help me with my taxes. I would get a small refund from the federal government but I had to pay state taxes.

18 April 1991

I spent the day in database computer training. I am beginning to get the hang of it.

After work I met with Greta Esposo and we went to Seoul International School to set up for our presentations. Seoul International School is a private school for grades kindergarten to 12. The tuition is $8,000 a year. It is a fabulous facility. They own their own fleet of about a dozen buses. I saw students being chauffeured home from school.

19 April 1991

The day was a very long one. It was Educator's Day. There was an opening session that featured a black high school speaker from Taegu American School. He was excellent. I gave my *Role of Masks in African Culture* presentation. I provided for about twenty participants, but there were more. There were about seven from my school in attendance. There were people of different nationalities there, Koreans, Indians, etc. There was a special luncheon for the presenters. We arrived back at base about 5 p.m. I ate very lightly because we were going to have the Shiny Apple Reception at the Embassy Club at 7 p.m. This reception honors those persons who give of their service to the school community. One recipient was a dentist that I learned was from Baltimore, Maryland, my hometown. He attended Dunbar High School.

20 April 1991

I headed for school about 8:55 a.m. to set up for the fifth grade rummage sale and bazaar. There was a nice size crowd, but we expected more. We sold about twenty-two tables at $10.00 each. The fifth graders also sold clothes, sodas and baked items. I saw about four of my pupils. Afterwards, I went to T.E.A.K. meeting where my name had been placed on the ballot for vice president.

I then went to the hairdresser. I was elated when the beautician told me that I had new growth. I had increased my vitamin E intake and I used a scalp ointment containing vitamin E, plus I get a deep conditioning treatment.

I went to the Embassy Club to the Kappa's dance. This crowd was a little different, somewhat low-keyed. The hard stompers were up at Osan Air Base where the Omegas were having a dance. I met a fellow by the name of Herman who had only been in Yongsan one week. Rosa had already met him. She said she knew 85% of the men on post. I believe her. She not only spoke to every other man, but she hugged everyone.

This week Tom Bradley, mayor of Los Angeles, is visiting Korea to foster improved trade relations.

21 April 1991

I went to service at 121 Evacuation Hospital chapel. Edna sang a solo. Rosa was also there. After this service we went to Gospel Service. The young children sang without a pianist and they did the best they could. Elder Jonah Ball was quite lengthy. We went to Main Post to the Moyer Recreation Center where the winners of the Earth Year Photo contest were honored. Edna Edwards won third place and honorable mention for her photos *Fries* and *Bird*. They were both snow scenes. AFKW TV was there and a reception followed. Edna was a star. She received 2 certificates and $50.00. I met the director of Camp Red Cloud's Arts and Crafts Center. He has been in Korea for twenty years.

22 April 1991

It is about 8 weeks before the end of school.

I held my 18th calligraphy class. We spent the time putting up a bulletin board display of the students' work in the main building.

Afterwards, Selena and I went to the transportation office to set up a pick-up time for our items which will be shipped to the States. I noticed that there was an error on my orders. It had authorized 100 pounds of weight to be shipped from Lorton to South Korea rather than from South Korea to Lorton. I made an appointment to go back on Friday.

Tony Nix called me. He wanted to stop by on Wednesday. He said he would call me at 5:30 p.m. I don't intend to answer the phone.

23 April 1991

It was a nice, sunny day. The temperature reached 72 degrees. There was nothing special today. There was no mail for me. Fred fell asleep again. I walked for an hour after work and I sent another box home containing my ice bucket, vases, jewelry, etc.

24 April 1991

I didn't go to work because I had to go to the hospital for a biopsy. The biopsy, performed by Dr. Marshall Smit, was rather uncomfortable. He ordered me to have a blood test and wrote me a prescription for multiple vitamins at my request. I received the report of my mammogram and it was good. I would have to have another in a year.

I returned home and picked up two boxes to mail at the post office. I found out that if I put a copy of my orders in the box, customs will not compel me to pay taxes on the items. The postmaster will stamp it *official* and they won't even open it.

I went to school to check my mailbox and to check on my classroom. The results of my children's tests were in. I was pleased. Fred scored the lowest, almost zero. Rosa called me into her office to tell me that Fred had moved the hands of the clock forward ten minutes so the substitute dismissed the children ten minutes early, so Rosa suspended him.

25 April 1991

I left school at 2:10 p.m. I came home so disgusted. I had to prepare schoolwork for Fred the first thing because he was on in-school suspension. Then I had to track Carl Albridge down to find out what was happening with Fred as far as his testing and screening. Then I got a call from Audrey's mother complaining that some boys were teasing her and had broken the handle on her lunch box. The boys were calling her "cockroach" and Wade went as far as to bring in a can of Raid to spray her seat. In questioning them, I found that Audrey was not completely innocent either and that Cheryl Barns broke her lunch box, not the boys.

I was also directed to get a roll of toilet tissue for my boys to keep in the classroom and dispense it to the boys as needed. Like Hell!! I was not toting toilet tissue for any 11-year-old boys. Tough luck!

The class couldn't watch a video because the cable was off and the media center was no help. Besides that, a military nurse came to talk to the girls about sex education/human growth and development.

26 April 1991

The day was a nice sunny, bright one. I hadn't planned to do much teaching. T.J. and Kirk Barry spent the day with the Earth Day activities. About six children were in counseling. Fred stayed awake. There was so much going on he couldn't sleep. We recited and recorded poetry. We had our spelling bee and Ben won. I gave him a small silk print that I purchased in Okinawa.

After work I went to the moving office to set a date to have 100 pounds of my belongings shipped home. They would not give me a pick-up date because the orders said to ship from Lorton to South Korea, and not from South Korea to Lorton. I was so disgusted that I stopped to buy some junk food, then on to Bentley's for "Happy Hour" and from there to Hartell House for another "Happy Hour."

27 April 1991

I went on a tour with some of my co-workers. It was another lovely day. The sun shone brightly. The base was beautiful with its foliage and flowers. Just about all of the school buildings and our bachelor officers quarters have been painted.

I went to school to record grades on three sets of papers that I checked last night. I then went to the parking lot to board the tour bus. We stopped first at Camp Market's Junkyard where surplus and outdated equipment was brought. We saw some things we could use at school.

From there we took a tour of the Port of Inchon. It is a magnificent port with eight harbors on the Yellow Sea. They also have locks that open and close from one side to the other rather than the two open gate type that I've seen in the Algiers Locks in Louisiana and the Erie Locks at Erie Lake. General MacArthur landed here in the 1950's. Also, Mrs. Park's husband designed the locks. Mrs. Park is our Korean culture teacher.

Our next stop was Freedom Park where there is a large statue of General Douglass MacArthur. It was a very lovely place. School children were there in uniform; senior citizens were doing a Korean ritual dance in a gazebo; fortune tellers told fortunes along the path; and young people frolicked about.

A good time was had by all. On the way back we saw a Korean woman with a basket of food atop her head. She was at the opening ceremony for a new building. She chased around in an effort to ward off evil spirits.

28 April 1991

I awoke this morning, had breakfast and worked on my last assignment for the Study of Teacher Training Course. I then went to service at South Post chapel. The minister's text came from John 15:1-8 which deals with love. There are two more Sundays before Mother's Day. The choir sang *Nearer My God to Thee* which is often sung at funerals. It was sad. I decided as I walked home that I would not attend Mother's Day service this year. It would be too painful having lost my mother less than a year ago.

I came home, had a light meal, then went to school to meet with other teachers and parents. We were going to Mount O'Pines to tour and plan for our three day camping trip on May 22, 23, and 24th. It was a very pleasant day and everything went well. We rode through parts of the city where I had never been. We passed the Blue House (the President's house) which is concealed by a high wall.

I watched the movie, *The Samaritan,* about Mitch Snyder, activist for the homeless. At the end he said, "When you see homeless persons, don't pass them by, speak to them, get them something hot to drink, or something to eat, smile or look in their eyes for you are looking in the mirror."

29 April 1991

We have about six more weeks in school. The class was awfully noisy. We had a storyteller who told two stories and an accomplished musician from New York. This assembly lasted almost an hour.

I checked my mailbox and found a letter from Beth. I guess I shouldn't be so critical, but be thankful that she wrote me. The letter opened on a morbid note. It read, "How are things? Mr. Theodore Gross, your former teacher died, also Mrs. Sarah Bundy, your piano teacher. Your old school was torn down. Mrs. Laura McDaniels, a former teacher, died as a result of a child pushing her down the steps as she was trying to break up a fight She had been teaching for forty-four years."

Calligraphy club was canceled because of the planned demonstrations in all the Korean cities. The university students were protesting the killing of a 20-year-old university student by four plain-clothes policemen. The policemen were charged and the police chief replaced. I guess the students wanted blood.

Selena drove me to the transportation office where I made an appointment to have 100 pounds of my belongings shipped to the U.S. My pick-up date is May 12th at 2:30. My things should reach Cameron Station, Virginia, on June 12th. When I reach home, I will call to have my things delivered to my house. I sent Tavia a copy of my orders to return home then back to Korea.

30 April 1991

This is the last day of April, which leaves about a month and a half until the end of the school year. The day was a pleasant one. I rearranged the desks yesterday so the children were excited about that.

After school we had our monthly faculty meeting. A large spread of food was brought in and we ate and ate and ate. I avoided all deserts except the bread pudding. This meeting was followed by a meeter-greeter-meeting. I expressed my concern that no one was at the airport to greet me and the fact that I had such a sorry sponsor. After having her son, Fred, in my class and after meeting her, I could understand why.

I went home, paid my cleaning lady, ate lightly and took my daily walk. I saw Dr. Smit on the street and he told me my biopsy was normal, so there's no need for a follow-up. That was good news. I returned home, wrote up an assignment for my last Study of Teacher Training class, then prepared to go to dinner at the invitation of Dora Johns.

We were joined by three very rich Korean women, one of whom was Dora's English student. The student paid the bill. Teaching Koreans how to speak English is big business here. It was a delightful evening.

1 May 1991

It is the first day of May, but it doesn't seem like it. It is so chilly that I have to wear a light coat.

The class is extremely noisy, so much so that I have to shorten the review lesson for the social studies test.

Keith's mother brought him to school. He said he was sick, but then she found out that Keith didn't want to come to school because some boys were threatening to beat him up.

2 May 1991

The day is still chilly. I went to work and rearranged the desks. I placed the well-behaved pupils on one side of the room and the misbehavers on the other side. I had to keep David Lee, who didn't go to camp with his class. He was an innocent, slow child. Fred, of all people, was trying to pick on him and did I light into him. Fred tried to doze off, but I stopped him.

I had the class make coats-of-arms. They did a fantastic job. After work I went to meet with Rosa and a group of teachers to review and revise the teacher handbook. Rosa volunteered us to work on the handbook when there was a committee already in place. Sally Jost went to Mrs. Knoy, our principal, to report it.

3 May 1991

Friday! the week seemed to have passed quickly. Fred made a nasty remark this morning, so I called his father. His father and mother came to school during lunchtime.

After work, I went to Dragon Hill Lodge for the opening ceremonies for Asian-American Week. The food was delicious and the entertainment was very good. Vance Millo was there. His sister danced. They are from Guam. Base Commander Colonel Franklin spoke or should I say read. He held his head down the entire time, never once looking at his audience.

I left there about 5:45 p.m. because I had to get ready to go to the Friendship Symphony Concert at the Seoul Arts Center Concert Hall. It was great. There was a pianist, a soloist, a flutist and the City of Inchon Chorus. The chorus sang the *Battle Hymn of the Republic, America, the Beautiful, Jennie with the Light Brown Hair,* and for an encore, *God Bless America.*

4 May 1991

This day is a beautiful day. I slept quite late, awaking about 8 a.m. I didn't rush. I went to the hairdresser and from there I went to school to bring home some things I had left there on Friday. As soon as I arrived home I received a call from Torri Bennett, a fourth grade teacher, who told me a child's father was looking for me because his father-in-law passed and they would have to leave to go to Bangkok and he wanted his daughter's schoolwork. I called and had him and his daughter meet me at school. I found a sympathy card for them and went to school. He was very appreciative. I left school and took my daily walk. Before coming home, I stopped at Pagoda Park down the street from my apartment where the teachers were having a picnic. I stayed just a short while because I had to get home to prepare to go to Tammi's. She picked me up at 5:30 p.m. When we arrived at Tammi's, Rosa Ridgely, her two guests and the Gonzalez's were there. We were first served pina coladas, then a New Orleans dinner. New Orleans is where Tammi and her husband, Raymond, are from. We had gumbo, jumbalaya, rice, red beans, macaroni salad, French bread and lemon pie. We talked and Jean and I shared our photo albums. Jonathon Hall, one of my fifth graders, was there. We went up on the rooftop to enjoy the view, but it was so chilly that we didn't stay long.

Soon after I arrived home, the phone rang. It was Tavia informing me that Marian, my oldest sister, had passed. Marian had been suffering with cancer for a number of years.

I then called Texas to talk to Amira, my niece. She told me that Marian had died in the hospital. She had begun to deteriorate and death seemed inevitable. John, her husband, was with her until about 7 p.m. Friday night. Marian passed about 5 a.m. Saturday morning. I called Edna who advised me to call Dr. Ellsworth pertaining to emergency leave. Marian was good to me. She was strong to the end.

5 May 1991

Edna called about 7:30 a.m. to tell me that she would stop everything to give me any assistance I needed. Dr. Ellsworth, superintendent, called me a little after 8 a.m. as he said he would. I put on my jogging suit and went for my daily walk. The air was pleasant and the streets bare. I returned and talked to Tavia. I told her that she had to call Red Cross so that I can get emergency leave to come home. Edna stopped by and brought me a coin from chapel service and informed me that the congregation offered a prayer in my behalf.

I went to school to finish planning for the week. I returned home to do some last minute things, and to reflect on the good times Marian and I had shared. I read the last letter that I received from her, dated March 23, 1991. Marian was so supportive and was always glad to hear from me. She had a great concern for the family and the relationship that existed between Beth and the rest of the family. Marian was a great mother, a loving wife and a super sister. She carried her hurts strongly and quietly; her son's skin disease, the death of her son at age 16, her own bouts with cancer and her operations. She bore them all in stride. She never complained. She lived a simple life and I believe she was content. She lived to see her daughter receive great honors, to be well employed and lastly, to wed. Her death will leave a void in John's life. I remembered how he grieved for his son.

6 May 1991

I arose at 5 a.m. in anticipation of going to the States. Edna drove me to the bus station to get a bus to Osan Air Base where I hoped to get a flight to Travis Air Force Base in Oakland, but there was only one seat and it was taken by a soldier on duty. I returned to Seoul, checked with the airline regarding a commercial flight to the States. Flying commercial, I won't get to Texas until Tuesday evening. I plan to call Amira and John and plead with them to hold the funeral on Wednesday.

I called Amira. She said she would get back to me after she and John made arrangements. She called me at 6 a.m. our time to say that the burial would be at 12 noon on Tuesday. I decided I would go to Texas anyway because I had emergency leave, I doubted if I could have worked this week under the circumstances and I wanted to be with Amira, John, Ada and Roy. I would see that we keep the bond that we had while Marian was alive. I just wanted to be there.

7 May 1991

I got up after I talked to Amira. I ate breakfast, wrapped a package to send home and prepared to leave for Texas. Paula called to give me her blessings and to ask when I wanted her to take in my newspapers.

I made arrangements to go to San Antonio and to return to San Francisco for an overnight layover. I plan to stop to see Gerald. As I had time, I went into the beauty salon to get my nails done. As I was leaving the salon, who should I run into? Beatrice Knoy, the principal. She said she was concerned about me. I was concerned that she wasn't at work. I took a cab to the Main Post and boarded a bus to Kimpo Airport.

I was early, so I read my newspaper and had a cup of coffee.

The Northwest Airline plane was very crowded. We touched down in Los Angeles at about 9:50 a.m. I went through customs, then checked in at America West Airlines. I had never heard of them, but the receptionist informed me that they had been in business for seven years. I called Gerald and informed him that I would stop to see him on my way home on Friday. The flight to Phoenix, Arizona, was about two hours. I went right to my next flight which took me to San Antonio. The flight over the desert and mountains was fascinating. I touched down in San Antonio at 6:38 p.m. I took the *Super Van* to the Greyhound bus station. I called John, then boarded a bus to Sequin at 8:45 p.m. John, Amira and Peggy were waiting for me. When I got to the house, Ada and Roy were there. We ate and talked and talked. John was very strong and he talked about his conversation with Marian and how she had prepared herself for death. Her memory will be with us forever. Her death had already become a reality when she was not at the airport with John to meet me.

I read the funeral program and in reading I noticed that she and John had been married on the same day that Daddy passed, September 24th. They were married on September 24, 1955, and Daddy died on September 24, 1975. I noticed, too, that the scripture on the program was the same as the framed verse that she had in her china closet.

8 May 1991

Today is Tia's third birthday. I awakened early but remained in bed. Ada brought me in some coffee. Amira came in and talked awhile with us. She said if there were any of Marian's clothes that we wanted we could take them. We were amazed at how many clothes Marian had, four closets full. There were even some that she hadn't worn. Tags were still on them. We all took several pieces for ourselves, Tavia, Joyce and Beth. We spent most of the day doing that.

9 May 1991

I awakened about 7:10 a.m. Peggy and I talked again. Ada joined us. She brought us some coffee and toast. We found a recent picture of Marian and I photographed it. I also photographed the many floral plants that she received.

10 May 1991

I said a sad good-bye to John, but I wasn't pleased with the very short good-bye. He was in tears.

I had a great flight to California. We crossed the snow-capped Rocky Mountains. Upon my arrival, I called Gerald. I then waited about an hour and a half for a shuttle to Oakland where I met him. From there, we took a bus to his apartment. Gerald and I talked and exchanged information. He gave me two Mother's Day cards containing money.

11 May 1991

I stayed awake most of the night because I didn't want to oversleep. I got up at 5 a.m., dressed, and we were on our way to the hotel to get the shuttle to the airport. We arrived at the airport at 6:12 a.m. The shuttle van was there. We were very early, but I got on the shuttle anyway. I don't trust California's traffic.

Incidentally, on the way to Oakland, the shuttle driver took us on a round about way to avoid the heavy traffic. In the process we got a great tour of the San Francisco Bay area. It reminded me a little of Korea with the houses on the mountainside.

I arrived at the airport and checked in right away. I was finished by 7:14 a.m. My flight wasn't until 10 a.m. I was sad, because I thought Gerald and I could have had breakfast together. So I had breakfast alone.

The flight was twelve hours and forty-six minutes long. It was long, long, long, but I arrived safely in Korea and that is all that mattered.

Transportation would not pick up my things to ship to the States while I was away because I was not there. I needed to have a power of attorney for Selena to release my belongings.

13 May 1991

I received several sympathy cards and words of condolence. I also received a card and a letter from Sarah Cane, a neighbor in Virginia, whom I had not heard from all year. That's just like her. She said she had seen Tavia and Tia and she praised me for doing such a fine job with Tavia and Gerald. I, too, am proud of them. Tavia graduated from St. Mary's University in Texas in 1981.

I had my last calligraphy club meeting, so I submitted my voucher for my pay. I then met with Rosa Ridgely who reported to me that Fred was sent to her again for misbehavior. I called his mother who felt that he shouldn't be sent to the office.

14 May 1991

The day went well. Fred didn't fall asleep. I received my N.T.E. scores. I scored average in two areas and high in the third.

After work, Selena and I went to Main Post to set up another appointment for our 100 pound shipment pick-up. It was crowded so we plan to go back tomorrow. She and I went on to Main Post. I went to the bank, picked up my photos at the PX and purchased plane tickets to fly to Pusan for our T.E.A.K. meeting on Saturday. I then returned home, had a light meal and started my schoolwork when Dora Johns of our social committee and her little son came by to bring me a large beautiful plant as an expression of sympathy. After they left, I took my daily walk.

15 May 1991

The day is a warm sunny one. Nothing unusual happened. Fred tried to doze off again, but I caught him. Gloria Bradley, the special education teacher, showed me his test scores and they were pitiful. The child needed some direction. His parents chastised him and spoiled him at the same time. I had been informed that they had problems, too, including a love triangle which resulted in a fight at the PX, slashing of tires, police records, etc.

I had to call Audrey Youngston's mother. Audrey has asthma, plus she is slow, a liar and a troublemaker. Her mother is concerned about her welfare on the camping trip next week and so am I. I am concerned not only about Audrey, but other problems I have in my class.

After work, I went with Selena to the transportation office to set up another appointment for pick-up of the items I am sending to the States.

16 May 1991

I awoke this morning very ill. I was weak, stiff and in pain. I forced some breakfast down, but shortly afterwards, I vomited everything up. After I felt I couldn't make it, and it was seven o'clock, I called the school for a substitute. I requested that the substitute call me later in the day. He did. It was Tammi King's husband, Raymond.

I stayed in bed all day and ate nothing.

17 May 1991

I awoke feeling stiff and weak, but with no pain, so I forced myself to go to work. I ate a little breakfast. I felt I had to go because Raymond King is not the best substitute. Sure enough, when I got to school, he had not followed my reading lesson, said the needle on the record player was broken. I guess he didn't think to borrow one from another teacher. He also said the class went wild during math. He had no control over the class whatsoever.

Edna stopped to bring some arts and crafts material that she would not need. She was transferring to Cuba to be closer to her mother.

I checked my weight at Moyer Recreation Center and found that I had lost five pounds from eating so little the past two days. I needed to lose the weight, though.

I went to school to pick up some work. I returned home and picked up a box to take to the post office to send home. I've spent a lot of money sending boxes home. Tavia must be tired of picking them up. I have about three more to send.

19 May 1991

I decided to go to South Post chapel. The minister told the congregation if they know of anyone with a drinking problem to please refer them to AA and then to the church. I thought about Beth, my sister. Ada and Peggy said that she was still drinking heavily. I had started writing a letter to her expressing my concern, but put it aside. The minister's statement prompted me to take it out, rewrite it, add to it and to send it off to her. I made up my mind to send the letter, even if she sent it back, called me up and cursed me out or wrote me a derogatory letter. Everyone talks about her drinking and how bad and unhealthy she looks, but they won't reach out to her because they are afraid to. I have grown stronger and I feel it a challenge to reach her. Beth has been a teacher for over thirty years and she deserves a better life.

I returned home, relaxed awhile and changed clothes to go the T.E.A.K. meeting which started at 4:30. I am officially the vice president of the Teacher's Education Association of Korea. The meeting was lengthy. It lasted until 7 p.m.

20 May 1991

The day was a very pleasant one. The weather was great. The children were as noisy as ever. Jonathon announced that Audrey Youngston's first name was Cock and last name was Roach, so I had him to write her name over a hundred times so that he would know and use it only.

I weighed myself at Moyer Recreation Center. I had managed to keep my five pounds off.

I called John about 7 a.m. this morning. He said he was doing well. He had gone to the hospital last Sunday, as he said he would, to thank the doctors and nurses at Audie Murphy Hospital for the way they treated Marian. He said they were both delighted and surprised. They even hugged him. He also said I had received some sympathy cards from my school and that he would bundle them up to send to me. He also said that Amira would come to Sequin on Tuesday because they needed to meet with the lawyer.

21 May 1991

The day is another very fine day. We went to the bowling center. It was free and we had fun. I bowled one game. The manager, Mr. Brighton, was strict, but nice. The pupils were allowed to buy drinks, but no food. Three pupils disobeyed and bought sweet buns.

Crystal Canty irked me by bringing kool-aid and spilling it on the floor. Mr. Brighton made her clean it up. To boot, she proceeded to distribute it to her classmates on the way back to school. I wrote her mother, a fellow teacher, a note. She was furious and told Crystal and me so. She was so angry that she didn't want to allow her to go on the 3-day camping trip.

22 May 1991

This is the first day of our 3-day camp-out. When I got to work everything was in order. The children came in ready and raring to go and so were the parents. I gave directions and then had them watch two sound filmstrips on food and you. They used the restrooms, then we went to the buses. Mrs. Millo, Ms. Martin, Mrs. Coleman, Mr. Hend, Mr. and Mrs. Neven, and Mrs. Pearse were there. Prior to leaving the classroom, Fred was in tears because his parents hadn't come. He was only to go on the condition that his parents accompanied him. He called home and they weren't there. They were at the buses. One bus was used to carry the luggage, food, and supplies. The Nevens, Fred's parents, rode on it.

We were on our way. The children were ready. They sang on the way up to the camp. When we arrived we met in a group to give directions. Dora Johns was very concerned that Dolly Davis was running the *show*. Dora said that Dolly led the parent planning meeting. She had not given us the schedule of activities nor the groupings. She even held the children's name tags. When children and parents asked us questions we could only respond, "I don't know." "I haven't the slightest idea." "Ask Mrs. Davis." We then proceeded to have the children unload the bus and to give them their cabin and group assignments. They also brought their own lunch and ate just before unloading the bus. There were enough parents for each cabin so I had my own, away from the others. It was a little scary out there alone, but I said a prayer for protection and braved it. I was responsible for tie-dying which I loved. Each of the 110 shirts turned out perfectly. We planned 3 sessions of activities for the afternoon. We then had a snack and games, then prepared for dinner which consisted of chicken, potatoes, rolls, carrots and cole slaw. It tasted delicious and the dining hall manager was well organized.

Afterwards, the children went to their rooms to prepare for their skits. At 7:30 we all met at the dance hall in the girls' quarters for soda, popcorn, cookies and dancing. They had a ball.

The music was just right. Also each group had to make up a song to sing after each meal.

At about 9 p.m. everyone was to return to their rooms and have lights out at 10 p.m. Some groups were so energetic that the parents either took them outside for story telling or took them on a night hike. I heard one group was up until 1:30 a.m.

23 May 1991

I walked over to the girls' quarters. Dora Johns and I were outside when Dolly Davis showed up. She said she felt some uneasiness. So we expressed to her our feelings about not being a part of the planning and not being informed of activities ahead of time. She said she thought she should do it because we had other things to do which was a flimsy excuse. Then she asked the silly question, "Do you all want to run everything from now on?" The answer was "No one is running anything". Besides we wouldn't change horses in the middle of the stream. We would proceed as planned with some more participation on the part of Dora and me. Teachers had often said that Dolly didn't speak to them at work. She was quite moody.

At breakfast she decided to take a very, very low profile. I believe she was mad.

That night the children met in a camp ring and sang songs. One of the volunteers brought along his keyboard. Each group presented a skit. I thought the boys were better than the girls. There was some dancing. At this time we had a large campfire. We even had a cute presentation by the parents and volunteers. It was another great fun night!!

24 May 1991

I made it through the night with all of its eerie sounds. I was brave. There I was in a cabin all by myself in a country about 8,000 miles away from my home in the States. I prayed and prayed hard. I awakened before dawn, read my Bible and read a newspaper. Incidentally, upon arrival each adult was given a two-way radio. So I had that although I wasn't sure how to operate it.

I had one tie-dye session today. Crystal was in it. Of course, she complained as usual. She wanted a light blue shirt and Mrs. Nevens poured a little green in the blue because it was weak.

After this session the children packed and we had a cook-out of hamburgers, corn chips, cookies and punch.

The buses arrived at about 11 a.m. and we were ready. We returned to school at noon. Everyone was so tired. I had the class to write how the camp-out fulfilled their sense of science enrichment, cooperative learning and building self-esteem.

25 May 1991

The packers came at 9 a.m. before I could get dressed. They took about 30 minutes or so to pack my things. I then dressed. Afterwards, I went to Edna's to watch her pack out. It was quite an adventure. She had eighty! eighty! eighty! boxes which did not include her furniture and the fifty! fifty! fifty! boxes that the packers had to pick up from school and then some. She also had furniture and items stored in Germany. The packers came at 8:30 a.m. and worked until 12 noon, returned and worked until 6 p.m.

Daily warnings were flashed across the screen about Korean student demonstrations.

26 May 1991

I awakened to a very chilly, rainy morning. It rained most of yesterday, too. I was feeling very homesick and I wanted to call home, but I was afraid I might get some bad news, so I contented myself by working on an arts and crafts plaque. I was also busy sorting out and throwing away papers. I received my frequent flyer notice and I had accumulated over 20,000 miles with Northwest Airlines, so I am entitled to a free trip.

I attended South Post chapel service. Russ Corb, our

media center specialist, is retiring. This was his last Sunday at church. He sang the Penitence, the story of the Prodigal Son. It was beautiful.

27 May 1991

I awakened rather early and arose early, although it was a holiday, the Memorial Day Observance. I gave in to my homesickness and called Tavia. She said everything was going okay. She has been receiving my boxes. I have about three more to send.

I called to ask Edna if she wanted to go to the Memorial Service on Knight Field on Main Post. I then went for a short walk. I called Edna again for her answer. She said she would meet me at 9:30 a.m. The ceremony was beautiful and solemn. I talked with Base Commander Will Franklin and his wife and found out that they would be returning to Lake Ridge in Virginia. There were books of remembrance that listed the names of the over 33,000 men and nurses who lost their lives in the Korean War. The names were listed by city and state and in alphabetical order. There were many names from Baltimore, Maryland, but I didn't recognize any.

28 May 1991

The children have twelve more days of school. The day is a beautiful crisp one. The class was noisy all day. Fred fell asleep during math.

After work Selena and I went to the legal office to get power of attorney papers. I got two, one for Dora Johns here in Seoul and the other for Tavia in Virginia.

I returned home, picked up a package and a box to mail to the States.

29 May 1991

I went to work and at 9 a.m. I had a screening meeting with Fred's parents. His mother still argued that her son doesn't have a peer relation problem. I allowed her to maintain her stance because I knew better and I wasn't going to argue with her.

I checked my mailbox and there was a lovely, comforting letter from Reverend Patterson and the Alston Street Baptist Church family. There was also a collection of the church bulletins including the one that announced Marian's passing.

30 May 1991

Before school this morning we had a pot luck breakfast for Russ Corb, the media specialist who is retiring. The breakfast was delicious and quite a spread of food. I abstained from eating any sweets.

I took a box to the post office to mail. I must have spent a couple hundred dollars in sending boxes home.

31 May 1991

This is the last day of May, Edna's birthday and Tammi King's anniversary. The day went well. We had a field day which lasted for one-and-a-half hours. Fred took first place in the frisbee throw competition.

I got ready to go to Judy's, a teacher friend, birthday party at the Embassy Club. It was a funny party. The only thing provided was popcorn and the birthday cake. You had to buy your own drink. It so happened there was food at Happy Hour inside and the party was on the patio. The food included veggies and dip, finger sandwiches, Swedish meatballs. Dr. Ellsworth, the superintendent of schools, was also at the birthday party. I stayed at the party for about an hour-and-a-half.

1 June 1991

The day is a lovely one. I checked some papers at home, then went to work to record the grades and to average some grades for my report cards. I also cleaned out a few drawers. I returned home, picked up some things and then I went to the commissary to buy a few items. I took the bus there and walked back. Upon arriving home, I was too tired to do much, so I relaxed. Edna called me about 2 p.m. to ask if I would come over to oversee the packers putting the boxes on the truck. I returned home and relaxed for I was going to a formal dance at the Embassy Club. I wore a black dress. The affair was in good taste. Three scholarships were awarded: two to blacks and one to a Korean girl. The music was old favorites. The food was great. Crystal's parents were there. I left about 12 midnight. As usual, I danced and danced and danced.

2 June 1991

This is a beautiful Sunday morning. I watched a gospel church service on T.V. before going to South Post chapel. It was a communion service. After service I returned home and worked on my report cards then went to Main Post to Moyer Center to the high school art show only to find that it wasn't there. I ran into Selena and she drove me back home to get my invitation. I found that it was at the library so we went there. It was a great showing of youth art work. From there we went to Whispers' in Dragon Hill. Selena was quite depressed because her son had called in the morning to tell her that her house had been flooded due to a sewage backup. Her son was able to call a friend in South Carolina who will try to help. I returned home where I stayed for the evening. As I got out of the car I ran into Edna who invited me to dinner and the theater with her and a friend.

3 June 1991

Fred fell asleep this afternoon despite the noisy class. I had them to write a composition titled *How to Behave the Week Before School Closes.*

Afterwards, I called the finance officer to find out if he had my paperwork in order for depositing my check in Virginia. Transportation also called to let me know that my ticket was ready and to find out where Lorton, Virginia is.

I came home, changed clothes, and took my daily walk. I then went to Oasis for a light meal. Oasis is nice about this time, 4:30 p.m., before the dinner crowd comes in. It is so relaxing and the food is reasonable. I ran into Tyrone. He's a trip. He claimed he had a Mercedes in D.C. and plenty of money. Really?

I proceeded to the shoppette to get some juice and headed for home. I enjoy my evenings in my apartment. It is so comfortable and relaxing.

4 June 1991

Another lovely day. We had the breakfast that we planned for our health unit. Fred brought in four large rings of sausage uncooked. Vance brought his sausage in cooked, sliced and ready to serve on a plate. Audrey didn't bring in the cereal she promised to bring. She did, however, have a sandwich bag full of cereal for about two people. She said she forgot it. All in all, everything went well. There was enough for all. Afterwards, we planned for our picnic on Friday.

After work, I went with Selena to the American Embassy to renew her passport. The Embassy is under tight security. We saw the riot squads throughout the city. We were able to get a ride back with two soldiers. The American fellow drove as wildly as the Koreans.

5 June 1991

Another beautiful day weatherwise. The class was noisy as usual. They came in with some silliness about, "You be my slave. How many slaves do you have?" I went to see Rosa for my evaluation. There was one point I didn't agree with her on.

6 June 1991

The weather is holding up nicely. When I got to school Edna told me that she forgot to tell me that my phone had been disconnected. I was shocked and angry. I requested that it be disconnected from June 17th through August 17th. I attempted to call the phone company, but it was not open. I proceeded to Rosa's office to express my concern for an item she had checked me on as "Satisfactory." She told me to write a paragraph explaining what I had done regarding the standard.

As luck would have it, my children had to take a reading

test, so that allowed me time to respond to Rosa's rating of me. I wrote three pages of explanation. When Amy Smart, the language specialist, came in to teach my class I went to the main building, xeroxed my writing, put it in an envelope and gave it to Rosa. I then called the telephone company.

The day wore on. Fred's mother came in and interrupted my class. Then, her husband came. They wanted to know what Fred had to bring for the picnic tomorrow. This eleven-year-old was the only child who couldn't deliver the message home.

There was no mail in my post office box, but in my school mailbox was a large gift. I took it out and opened it right away. It was a birthday gift from Selena, a sectional Korean container. That brightened my day.

I walked to the telephone company and waited about a half hour before things were cleared up. Some one failed to write the day the service requested was to be done.

7 June 1991

I approached Rosa about my evaluation and she said she couldn't see me until Monday, but she had made a change which she would explain to me.

When I went to my classroom, the children had begun to bring in items for the picnic. We had a social studies lesson, then walked to the high school for the 5th and 6th grade honor assembly. The children were really dressed up, the way they should have been on picture taking day. The assembly was nice. Colonel Will Franklin read his speech with his head down. His speech writer would have been ashamed of him because I certainly was. The other two speakers, Matthews and Nelson, were enthusiastic and informative.

After the assembly, I took the class back to the room, gave them an inspirational talk, then sent those who needed to do so to change their clothes for the afternoon picnic. Fred hadn't brought a change of clothes, nor the hamburgers he was supposed to bring.

He said his mother would bring them. Mind you, every child brought his own items and clothing. He began to cry because his mother hadn't arrived. I had him to call her at home at 11 a.m. She didn't answer, so he did cry. He cried on the way to the picnic and at the picnic. His mother finally arrived claiming she had to wait in line for 30 minutes to pay for the hamburgers.

When a water fight broke out, I took the class back to the school. That was about 1:20 p.m. Dora Johns's class picnicked with us. She had to leave, so Raymond King took over. She couldn't get any parents, so her husband sent three soldiers over to help supervise the students. The afternoon would have gone well back at school except I had to reprimand some pupils who had gotten noisy and Ben who pushed T.J.

I came home and relaxed, then prepared to go to dinner with Edna, a Korean fellow named Sam Pyo and a guest Korean young lady who had served as a missionary in Sudan. We had dinner at the Main Post Club. We left the club, and rode across town to the Seoul Art Center for the Seoul Lady Singers concert. It was great. It began with the singing of four Negro spirituals. I couldn't imagine Koreans singing Negro spirituals. They sounded as good as Fisk University or the Wings Over Jordan Choir. A humorous incident happened when a member of the maintenance crew came out to move the piano, the audience applauded him. It was a great evening.

8 June 1991

When I opened the door to pick up my newspaper there was a note from Edna asking me to call her ASAP, and so I did. She wanted me to help her with her Study of Teacher Training assignments. That was the last thing I wanted to do. So, I told her I would call her when I felt up to it.

I went to school to record some grades and to clean up, then proceeded to Hartell House. There was Rosa Ridgely's car parked in the parking lot of the Hartell House with a note attached which read, "This car is disabled. The owner is seeking help and can be located in Oasis Restaurant, Ms. Ridgely."

I continued my walk and as I passed the high school I noticed the crowd. It was the commencement exercise. It is a good feeling to be graduating and even better to receive honors. Students received scholarships ranging from $500 to $45,000. One student would go to West Point.

9 June 1991

This is a lovely Sunday, even though it is raining. I went to 10:30 a.m. Protestant service at South Post chapel. Afterwards, I came home, changed my clothes and went to school to work. I returned home, took a nap, then woke up and dressed to go to Beatrice Knoy's retirement reception at five. It was well attended. There was the receiving line of Rosa Ridgely, vice principal; Beatrice Knoy, principal; Dick Knoy, her husband, and Dr. Jim Ellsworth, superintendent.

There was a lovely cake and a large scroll for everyone to sign. A soldier, Sgt. Wilson, presented Beatrice with a citation and a medal from the U.S. Army. I left after about an hour and fifteen minutes. By now I am tired of parties and receptions.

10 June 1991

This day is the beginning of the last week of school. (I gave the class a math test.) Chloe Macklin, a fifth grade teacher, came over to bring me some things since she was moving to third grade. She also invited my class to come to her room to watch a video. We did so. Afterwards, we returned to the classroom for our spelling bee. I organized the children to deliver my books to my new room. Meanwhile, I received a phone call from a Family Service Unit representative asking questions about Fred Proctor. His parents were to meet with her at 2:30 p.m. They were thinking of sending him to Tripoli for testing. There was a possibility he has a sleeping disorder.

We went to Chloe's room to watch an afternoon video, *Land Before Time*. I checked my mailbox and there were quite a number of sympathy cards sent to Texas from colleagues, mail from Tavia, and mail from the OEA.

11 June 1991

There was news of a volcano eruption in the Philippines and Clark Air Base had to be evacuated. Violent storms struck Bangladesh and parts of Russia. These are trying times. I met with Rosa. She changed the standard rating to "Exceeds."

We had our spelling bee. Kirk Barry is champ and Henry Carn is runner-up.

After work, Selena and I went back to transportation. I can't pick up my new ticket until tomorrow. I had to change a stop on my ticket, Oakland to San Francisco. I picked up three prints I had framed. Then, Selena dropped me off at the hairdresser. The lights went out mid-way through getting my hair curled. Cha had finished my manicure. Susie continued to curl my hair by candlelight. The burner kept heat for quite awhile. Just about all electricity on base was out. The lights in the stairwell of my building were on. I guess they are on a different generator. When I returned home, I couldn't heat anything so I ate cold cereal and then took a nap. There was a knock at the door. It was Selena bringing some packages I had left in her car. She said many people went to Dragon Hill Lodge, which wasn't affected by the black-out.

12 June 1991

Today is the last full day of school for the children. They are indeed very hyper, but not as hyper as in the States. I presented Kirk Barry and Henry Carns a certificate for being spelling champions and one of my African motif plates. We then went to Mary Canty's room next door to watch a video but the picture was snowy, so we went to the next room, Nancy Benton's, and watched television. We also did some social studies this week. After lunch we watched *Sleeping Beauty*. Speaking of *Sleeping Beauty*, Fred fell asleep this afternoon.

13 June 1991

I was in no hurry to get to work because the students had to attend school. I turned in my report cards, paid Rosa for the Franklin dinner and turned in my plan and grade books.

I went to the staff breakfast. There was so much food, but I chose a little quiche, a half of boiled egg and fruit. Gifts were given to staff members who were leaving.

I went to my classroom and worked some more. I moved some things to my new room. Beatrice Knoy, the principal, came by to say good-by. She was retiring this year after forty years in education, twenty-eight of them in DODDS and eight of those years as principal of Seoul American Elementary School.

14 June 1991

This is the last day of school. The children reported for one hour and fifteen minutes. I had them to make a Father's Day card and to write one day's schedule by memory, then they played games. I received several gifts that I adored. Edna gave me a beautiful address book which I sorely needed because I had only address pages from a calendar book. Stacie gave me some Korean stationery. I was so happy because I wanted to buy some more before I left Korea. Ryan gave me a pen, Virginia, a necklace and earring set and Jeremy, a beautiful small ceramic container.

15 June 1991

Today I will go home to the States. I arose about 7 a.m., had breakfast, watched T.V. and read some poetry. I took another box to the post office. I debated whether or not to go to Chosun

Gift Shop and decided against it because it would mean I would have to wrap and send another box because my luggage is already heavy.

Selena called and we talked and said our good-byes, then she called back to ask if I wanted her to take me to the bus station. Was I glad. I took my luggage downstairs. I saw Ronda Golden so I hugged her good-bye. Selena was on time. She came exactly at 11:30 a.m. When we got to the bus station it was crowded. Others had the same idea because the bus to Kimpo Airport was free. A cab would cost $20.00. I was glad Selena was there. She ran to put my luggage in the storage part, while I dashed on the bus to get a seat.

I managed to get through customs okay although it was crowded. I couldn't get a no-smoking seat, so I settled for a smoking seat because I wasn't going to miss this flight! The guy who sat beside me had been drinking and was a chain smoker. He was reading a paperback. The way he kept ordering drinks, I don't know how he could concentrate on reading.

This flight was ten hours and thirty-nine minutes long. Most of the flight was bumpy, with much, much turbulence. We had to wait on the plane for ten minutes because customs was backed up. On the flight we watched *The Gipper*, *Alice* and a cartoon.

This was a flight to San Francisco. San Francisco is beautiful. There is a U.S. Naval Base there called *Treasure Island* which affords a lovely view of the bay with its sailboats, the city skyline and the bridge. When I arrived at San Francisco I took a van to Oakland, where I met Gerald who drove Mike's car. The last time I was in San Francisco, I waited an hour and a half for the van.

Gerald and I talked, then we went grocery shopping. I prepared two dishes when we returned to his apartment. While we were out, he showed me where he worked and the beach where one can get a scenic view of San Francisco.

16 June 1991

I awoke about 7 a.m., had breakfast, then prepared to go to church. We went to service at Faith Temple Baptist Church, where Reverend William Carson is pastor. It is located in Oakland. The church and service reminded me of Friendship Baptist in Baltimore and Rehobeth Baptist in Washington, D.C. The singing, prayers, and message were very good.

We left there and went to Parc Oakland Hotel where the California Northwest Baptist Convention convened. When we arrived at the convention, things were in full swing. Reverend Hamilton was preaching. The people were dressed very well. Hats and more hats! We went to the lobby where they were selling hats, jewelry, hose, clothes, tapes, robes, tambourines, health and beauty products, cookies and pens. It was very crowded. I have been to so many of these conventions before and I enjoy such services very much. Good singing, preaching and praying.

17 June 1991

I awoke at 3 a.m., went back to sleep, awakened again at 4:44 then 5:02 and 5:30 a.m., then stayed awake until 6:30 and went back to sleep until 9:35. I got up, dressed, had breakfast, and did my morning reading. I then watched TV until Gerald came home at 12:30. He ate lunch, rested and we walked back to his job. We stopped at the Bank of Alameda to change a large bill. Then onto his job where I met his supervisor, Dr. John Dyson, Toni, the person whom he was constantly in contact with from Virginia, several employees, Frances who invited Gerald to Thanksgiving dinner, Mrs. Halloman's son (Gerald stayed with Mrs. Halloman on 22nd St. awhile), Ted whom I met earlier and is an artist, the maintenance people and several other employees.

Gerald took me on a short tour of the facility. I photographed him at work, then sat at his desk to read some magazines, then I took a walk. I stopped at the yogurt store and purchased a cone of non-fat almond nut yogurt. I sat outside on the bench to eat it. I then decided to return to the Department of Agriculture building. I waited until Gerald finished his work. He had to allow some slides to dry, then we walked home. It was a beautiful day. We enjoyed the colorful Victorian houses with their lovely flowers and the tall palm trees.

18 June 1991

Today is much cooler. I got up about 7 a.m., had breakfast, got dressed and went to send off a box of my clothes.

19 June 1991

I awoke about 5:30 a.m. Gerald was getting ready for work. He told me that he would call about 8:30 a.m. or 8:45 a.m. to let me know he was on his way back to his apartment. So I got up about 6:30 a.m. and prepared for my travels to Virginia. I was all ready at 8:45 but there was no call from Gerald so I called his job at 9:15. He was not there so I assumed he was on his way. At about 9:25 I looked out the door for him and there he was. He talked further about his car, then he and I prayed together. He drove me by his job to meet Sue who had just returned from Hawaii. She is a 22-year-old Hawaiian. I also met a lady who was in her office meditating. From there we went to Parc Oakland Hotel where I would take a shuttle van to the San Francisco Airport. Big Brothers and Big Sisters of America were convening so I walked around the exhibit hall.

The van was about ten minutes late. I bade Gerald farewell. Traffic wasn't bad going into San Francisco. The weather was great. I boarded Northwest Flight 28B, and sat in seat 21A. A lady and man, business persons, sat beside me. They worked on a project most of the way. We had to travel south to Albuquerque to avoid turbulent weather which made us about 25 minutes late arriving in Memphis. Our ground stay in Memphis was short. Before landing we were in a holding position because the airport was busy. Then on to Washington National Airport. We touched down at 10:45 p.m. It was quite a long taxi to the terminal. The inside area looked new. I had not been in National Airport in quite a while.

Tavia was not there, so I called Jenny to see if she was waiting over there. She was not. I called home and got her answering service. She arrived after I got my luggage and waited about 10 minutes. Tia was there looking very much as she did when I left her. I sat in the back of the car with her and we chatted on the way home. There appeared not to be any changes in the community.

When I entered the house some things were not in place. So my work began. I wasn't sleepy, so I worked cleaning, clearing, and rearranging the house until 4 a.m.

I plan to return to Korea in the fall to work. It was a big decision. I was happy there. I miss my family and friends, but it was a blessing for me and I enjoyed it. I hope Tavia and Gerald will visit me next year.

I looked forward to coming home and I look forward to returning to Korea in the fall.

I recall when I was in the States in December, America looked foreign, Korea was like home. The mind does strange things to people.

ABOUT THE AUTHOR

Ms. Goodwin has taught elementary school for many years. She holds a B.S. degree in elementary education from Coppin State College; MFA degree in art education from the Maryland Institute College of Art; and an Ed.D. degree in curriculum and instruction from Virginia Polytechnic Institute and State University. She served as vice president of the Teachers Education Association of Korea (TEAK). Her strong interest in art led her to study Oriental ink painting at Hong - ik University in Korea. She has traveled extensively throughout the United States, Asia and other parts of the world. She serves as a docent at the National Museum of African Art in Washington, D.C. One of her favorite pastimes is reading. She hopes to write her family history soon.

RE-ORDER FORM

To order additional copies of **FRESH MEMORIES,** complete the information below:

Ship to: (PLEASE PRINT)

Name:_____
Address:_____
City/State/Zip:_____
Day Phone:_____

__Copies of **FRESH MEMORIES,** @ $14.95 ea. $____
__Postage and handling @ $3.50 per book $____
   (VA residence) add 4.5% Tax $____
                  Total Amount Enclosed $____

Make checks payable to: Daisy W. Goodwin
Send to: Daisy W. Goodwin, P.O. Box 255
Lorton, VA 22199